Why HINDU Dharma is Under ATTACK by Muslims, Christians and the Left

Why HINDU Dharma *is* Under ATTACK *by* Muslims, Christians *and* the Left

A Collection of Essays

MARIA WIRTH

Vitasta

Published by
Renu Kaul Verma
Vitasta Publishing Pvt Ltd
4348/4C, Ansari Road, Daryaganj
New Delhi - 110 002
info@vitastapublishing.com

ISBN: 978-81-19670-65-9
©Maria Wirth
First Edition 2025
MRP ₹450

All Rights Reserved.
No part of this publication may be reproduced, stored in a retrieval system, or transmitted in any form, or by any means–electronic, mechanical, photocopying, recording or otherwise–without the prior permission of the publisher. Opinions expressed in this book are the authors' own. The publisher is in no way responsible for these.

Edited by Reena Singh & Renu Arya
Layout by Rohit Gautam
Cover Design by Smriti Maheshwari
Printed by Vikas Computer and Printers, New Delhi

Contents

Introduction	ix
Indian Wisdom They Fear	1
Basics of Vedic Wisdom	10
The Divine, Your Dearest Companion	16
The Misunderstanding That Killed	20
The Source of All is ONE	25
Drawbacks of Hinduism	28
Indian Wisdom and Modern Science	30
If Westerners Knew Facts about Hinduism	38
When Germany is Christian, is India Hindu?	43
Is Hindu Dharma Good, and Hindutva Bad?	48

Letter on Hinduism vs. Hindutva	51
Is Hinduism a Religion or a Way of Life?	54
The Young Acharya of Bageshwar	58
Miracles are Possible: My Experience	64
A Victory for Hindus after 500 Years of Struggle	67
Kanwar Mela in Haridwar	73
The Value of Bhajans (in Euros)	80
Is Buddhism Intellectual and Hinduism Superstitious?	83
Is there Rivalry Between Buddhism and Hinduism?	88
What is Religion Good For?	91
Please Hindus, Don't Say 'All Religions are the Same'	100
Are Christians Under Attack in India?	103
My Letter to Pope Francis	110
My Reply to an Indian Christian Politician's Tweet	117
An NRI who Converted to Christianity	120
Are there Good Reasons to Accept Christianity?	122
Are Jihadis to Blame for Attacking Us?	126
An Interview with a Would-be Jihadi	134
My letter to Zakir Naik	140

A Pakistani Woman's Concern for Hindus	148
Attacks on Hindus have an Agenda	152
Divisive Forces and Hateful Voices	160
A Strange Question on Quora: Is India becoming the most hated country?	166
No Place for Truth in Political Correctness	169
Rebirth is for Real—Within Maya	175
Amnesia of Animal Eaters	181
India's Holy Cows	187
The Caste Question	190
The Brahmin Debate	196
Dharma vs. Secularism	200
Indian Influence on German Philosophers	207
Should Indians Stress on Their Sufferings like Jews Do?	213
If Only All Humans had the Inclusive Hindu Mindset	220

Introduction

THE WORLD has changed significantly within the last few years. Many of these changes are very concerning, especially the casual talk by some politicians about the possibility of a nuclear war, and the dangers of artificial intelligence, which will not only render many jobless and possibly directly influence our thoughts, but may even go out of human control. Further, there is a big economic downturn in many countries and increasing censorship of speech. It seems as if the world is moving towards a China-type controlled one-world society.

In this scenario, social media is both a boon and a bane. It is a bane, when it keeps our attention, addictively, on scrolling for ever more information or entertainment, without giving us a break to be present in the here and now—the most important place and time of our life. And our phones may even lure us into debasing our life with violent computer games or pornography.

Yet, on the other hand, social media has also contributed greatly to waking people up to what is happening. 'Deep State' has become a household word. Mainstream media has lost the trust of many. Even science, academia, and medicine have come under scrutiny and do not look so good and innocent any longer. Too many claims, ridiculed by the media as 'conspiracy theories', have unfortunately been confirmed as true.

There is another, very positive aspect which gets traction, and that too, is thanks to social media platforms—more and more people are searching for the Truth—not merely questioning facts that are presented by the media, but searching for the big, transcendental Truth about God and themselves.

Many Westerners are going back to Christianity and declaring their faith in Jesus. Even a decade ago, it would have been inconceivable that Tucker Carlson, a big American influencer, would ask Russell Brand, a big British influencer, on stage to lead an audience of ten thousand in prayers.

I consider it a good development for Westerners. The erosion of belief in a Supreme Power was obviously planned—starting in Russia and China with communism and taking root in the West with the Hippie movement of the 1960s.

Now, there is a pushback against the agenda which wants us to identify only with the body, and focus only on sensual enjoyment, never mind how low that enjoyment may be. The Zeitgeist is changing, even though the elite still try to convince us that 'It is ridiculous to believe in a God or a soul' (a recent quote by the celebrated historian and author, Yuval Noah Harari who is a regular at the World Economic Forum).

Yet, I wish that people all over the world would know about Bharat's Eternal Wisdom, called Sanatana Dharma. Or rather, I wish they would know what this Eternal Wisdom is really about and not be influenced by false, mischievous claims by those who don't want this Wisdom to be known.

The reason: Sanatana Dharma is closer to the Truth than Abrahamic religions.

Devotion to God or Jesus or Allah is definitely helpful in life. But doubts may arise from time to time, because those religions are all about 'belief in a story' that happened several hundred years ago. It is all about 'thinking' and not about 'who or what enables thinking'.

Since ancient times, India was the 'Land of Wisdom'. Vedic wisdom is not based on belief in a story. It gives knowledge about the Absolute Truth and asks us to verify it by experiencing it within ourselves—true Self-Realisation.

The most important knowledge is: We are not small individuals in a big world, but are one with Brahman. And Brahman, though indescribable, is best described as limitless, blissful Consciousness, out of which, this world and everything in it, 'appears'. It means, the world and our small, individual selves are not solid. They are more like Virtual Reality, or in Indian terminology, Maya. What is 'solid' and really true is only our essence or self—Pure Consciousness.

When I heard this for the first time back in April 1980, at the Kumbh Mela in Haridwar—it immediately made sense to me. For the first time, I got convincing answers to questions that had troubled me since my teens. Questions like:

What is most important in life?

Is there a God?

Is death the end of me?

These questions were now replaced with the most important question:

Who am I really?

Yet, this question cannot be answered with words. It

needs to be 'known' within. The goal of our life is to realise the truth of who we are.

I wanted to dedicate my life to search for the Truth and stay on in India, because the country was just more conducive for spiritual search. Yet to do this, I needed a longer visa and earn some money.

So, in 1981, I wrote my first article—about insights I had gained while being in the presence of Sri Anandamayi Ma and other great spiritual personalities like Devaraha Baba, and from reading numerous books and sitting still for many hours in meditation. I felt that this precious wisdom, which is still alive in India, is lacking in the West.

I was fortunate. This first article was published in the German magazine *Psychologie Heute*; two other magazines reprinted it. The editor asked me to continue writing, as he had rarely seen such clarity regarding Indian Wisdom. He even gave me an advance for my next article—a report on a conference in Mumbai on 'The Convergence between Indian Wisdom and Modern Science'. Obviously, back then in 1981, India's Wisdom was appreciated.

During the first 20 years, I stayed in the 'spiritual Bharat' of ashrams, pilgrimage places, sadhus, and mainly met Indians who were connected to their roots. I thought that all Indians were like this. After all, their tradition and scriptural heritage is a treasure trove.

Only when I moved into a 'normal' environment in 2001, did I realise that Hindu Dharma is not only ignored in education, but also viewed negatively by the media and academia.

I realised only then that on the one hand, many Indians had converted to Islam and Christianity during the long foreign rule, and naturally, their new religion indoctrinated them into believing how bad their previous faith was. And, on the other hand, even many Hindus have no idea about their spiritual treasure. Especially the convent-educated Hindus who often dismiss their tradition as 'primitive', without knowing even a basic text like the Bhagavad Gita.

They are like those proverbial people who are sitting on a box of gold but do not know it, and instead go for artificial jewellery elsewhere.

This 'box of gold' has many aspects. The most important one is:

India has preserved the most profound philosophical and spiritual insights of the ancient rishis (sages), and their methods on how to fulfil one's life's purpose and how to be truly free and fearless.

Yet it seems, free and fearless people are unwanted in our times. Otherwise, it is hard to explain why the media and academia hardly ever mention anything positive about India. It almost seems as if they do not want to draw any attention to India, maybe because they fear that people might discover that great treasure.

This book is a collection of forty-three of my over 200 articles. Some are unchanged, like my letter to Pope Francis, who has meanwhile passed away, or my reply to Zakir Naik, a radical Islamic preacher. Many are updated or have otherwise been improved.

The main topics are:
- The truth about who we are, what is our purpose in life, and where can we discover true love and happiness.
- Some aspects of the living Hindu culture.

- How Hinduism[1] relates to Buddhism and to the Abrahamic religions.
- What is special in Hinduism—like Rebirth or the regard for animals.
- Why is Hinduism attacked so much?
- The great influence that India had on German philosophers.

In recent times, attacks on Hinduism have become very vicious. Hindu Gods are called demons not only by Christian missionaries but also by Western academics and certain Indian politicians who want the faith of the Hindus to be 'eradicated'.

There are mischievous attempts to associate Hinduism with dark satanic cults, whose existence in secret societies of the topmost global elite can no longer be ignored. Those cults are the complete opposites of the benevolent Sanatan (=Eternal) Hindu tradition.

Hinduism's focus is on a *dharmic* (righteous) life and, to overcome one's ignorance regarding this illusionary world and to realise one's true Self. In contrast, the focus of those satanic cults is on achieving pleasures, riches, and power in this ephemeral world, even if it requires selling one's soul to the devil.

Are the attacks on Hinduism an expression of the spiritual fight of the forces of darkness against the forces of light? Of the egoistic Asuras against the benevolent Devas?

---

1   I often use 'Hinduism', as under this term, given by the British, Sanatana Dharma or India's Eternal Vedic Wisdom is known the world over.

Bharat[2] is probably the only country in the world, where the Devas are worshipped every day in thousands of temples across this ancient, vast land.

And, Bharat is probably the only country in the world, where the knowledge about our essential divinity is still alive; and, where not only countless sadhus, but also many ordinary Hindus dedicate some time daily to connect with divinity.

The vicious attempts of reviling the Hindu tradition need to be countered. At the same time, the precious wisdom of the ancient Vedas, which uplifts and gives meaning to life, needs to be spread.

People will then realise that Hinduism is not what mainstream media, Western academia, or the clergy of Abrahamic religions want us to believe. Rather, it is our best guide to true fulfillment and love.

I hope this book contributes in spreading this profound knowledge and inspires readers to search for true love and happiness within.

PS: Since my mother tongue is not English, kindly excuse and overlook any flaws.

---

2 Bharat is the Indian name for India

Chapter 1

Indian Wisdom They Fear

HOW DID I reach the conclusion that certain forces do not want humans to know about Indian wisdom, and thereby want to prevent them from knowing about, and connecting with their divine inner being?

I figured this out by observing what has happened over time and especially in the last two decades.

When Vedic knowledge reached Europe over 250 years ago, it was praised as the greatest gift to humanity by philosophers like Voltaire and Schopenhauer. In the first half of the twentieth century, scientists, like Schrödinger or Max Planck, too, praised it.

Even as late as 1982, Fritjof Capra, physicist and author of *Tao of Physics*, presented at a conference in Mumbai, the new paradigm of physics in tune with India's wisdom. He said, 'All is interconnected, nothing is separate; all is one energy, our senses deceive us,' and added:

'In all likelihood, this energy is conscious.'
I was there and heard him say it. He got a standing ovation.

In the 1970s, when I was studying at Hamburg University, 'Self-Realisation, Enlightenment, Expanded Consciousness' were buzzwords. Indian wisdom was seen in a positive light. 'India shops' sprang up with books like *Autobiography of a Yogi* by Paramahansa Yogananda. Maharishi Mahesh Yogi and Osho attracted the youth.

The Church, unsurprisingly, didn't like the fascination of Western youth with Hindu thought and appointed 'Cult Observers'. They warned parents that their children will become mad if they fall for those Indian gurus. However, the Church could not prevent a huge loss of faith. The churches became empty. Indian wisdom was in vogue.

Yes, there were many, who misunderstood 'Indian wisdom' and copied only the long hair and the *chillum* of the sadhus, and not their wisdom and discipline. But generally, we Westerners felt India had something that was lacking in the West. It had wisdom about who we are and what is the purpose of our life. And, it also had a connection to a magical, supernatural dimension, which we so missed in the West.

In the 1970s, and even before that, Western researchers had studied the brain of Yogis, who had miraculous powers. Alice and Elmar Green come to mind. The US Army Intelligence was keen to exploit those powers, including materialisations from thin air. They also sent an army commander to the Bob Monroe Institute to learn how to have out-of-body experiences—for possible use in spying.

This commander, Wayne McDonnell, wrote an interesting, 31-page document in 1983. This report[3] was declassified by the CIA in 2003 and is available on the internet. It vindicates the Holographic theory of the Universe.

In point 34 of the report, McDonnell wrote:
> The classic description of a universal hologram is found in a Hindu sutra which says:

'In the heaven of Indra there is said to be a network of pearls so arranged that if you look at one, you see all the others reflected on it'.

He further writes:
> …it shows that the concept of the universe, which at least some physicists are now coming to accept, is identical in its essential aspects with the one known to the learned elite in selected civilizations and cultures of high attainment in the ancient world.

Remember, this was written in 1983, when Indian wisdom was still valued in Western intellectual circles, and when 'at least some physicists', like David Bohm or Fritjof Capra, had the courage to acknowledge those ancient insights. Meanwhile, this concept of the universe has disappeared from public view, though the Holographic theory has not been disproven. Has further research been done but without drawing attention to it?

---

3   Gateway Process Report: https://www.cia.gov/readingroom/docs/CIA-RDP96-00788R001700210016-5.pdf

In the late 1980s, another positive aspect about ancient India was discovered in the West: Newspapers reported that NASA has discovered that Sanskrit is the most perfect language. This was at a time, when Indian students generally found Sanskrit 'boring', and preferred to study French or German.

The points, which I just mentioned, show that Vedic wisdom was appreciated in Western academic circles even till some decades ago, though the British had been rather successful in making **Indian** academic circles look down on it and instead look up to the West.

From appreciation to vilification… Why?

Then, around the year 2000, something changed.

Personally, I got an inkling, when in 2001, the editor of one of the German magazines, to which I contributed, wrote to me:

"You must have noticed spirituality is out. Wellness is in."

No, I had not noticed.

Ever since, yoga and meditation are presented only as a means for physical and mental wellness. Their potential for *mukti* (liberation) from our ignorance about this world, is ignored or purposely kept hidden.

Indian wisdom—including the knowledge that this world is not the real thing but Maya (a kind of dream by Brahman)—went out of fashion.

Consistent with this trend, mainstream scientists now consider consciousness, unlike Fritjof Capra in 1982, as a kind of secretion from the physical brain, and mainstream philosophers consider consciousness as indistinguishable from its content. They seem to be unable to conceive of pure, thought-free consciousness—the Brahman of the Vedas which is the Absolute Truth—or are they not meant to disclose this Truth?

Nowadays, many in the West even declare that there is no such thing as truth, but claim, 'Everyone has his own truth!' Or, 'The goal of life is personal.' If you follow what is happening in the West regarding woke-ism, genderism, drag queens, etc., you wonder if common sense, virtues, and dharma have completely gone out of the window. The dark opening ceremony of the Paris Olympics in July 2024 was one such example.

However, after President Trump took office in January 2025, the woke agenda received a welcome setback. Trump signed executive orders that the US recognises only two sexes—male and female and also scrapped the DEI (Diversity, Equity, Inclusivity) programmes in the US Government.

Finally, Hindus started shaking off their colonial mindset.

Around the same time, in 2001, when my German editor wrote that 'spirituality is out', an important shift also occurred in India: Many Hindus started realising that their tradition is preferable and yes, superior, to Abrahamic religions. The internet facilitated this realisation and brought like-minded Hindus together.

In all likelihood, connected to this Hindu awakening and wanting to put an end to it, the Western media and Left academics now falsely and perfidiously accused Hindus, and especially Brahmins, of oppressing minorities and lower castes.

The verbal attacks on Hindus reached a dangerous level. Therefore, it is no surprise that Hindus came under physical attack even in England and America, apart from brutal attacks in Muslim countries, like in Bangladesh after the takeover of the government by Mohammad Yunus in 2024.

Conferences on 'Dismantling Global Hindutva' and 'Eradicating Hinduism' were organised abroad and in India, where Indians with Hindu names and even prominent politicians took part. I saw a video clip on Twitter (now X), where India was called 'a cursed land' and Indians 'disgusting, unhygienic creatures' and even worse.

Even Rahul Gandhi, in his first speech as leader of the Opposition, said something incredible on the floor of the House in July 2024—'Those who called themselves Hindus, only talked about violence, hatred, and untruth'. And to make a greater impact, he repeated 'violence, hatred, untruth'.

What is the agenda behind such fabricated accusations?

Who is interested in ensuring that the most inclusive faith and its followers become the target of hatred?

And why?

Why are there attacks targeting Hindus, generally a most tolerant and peace-loving community?

And, why this down-sizing of Yoga and meditation, ignoring its full potential of realising one's true Self?

It is indeed difficult to fathom.

The reason could be that there are still many Yogis in Bharat who have realised their true Self. It is easier for Hindus to understand the profound Vedic wisdom and touch their divine, inner core or *Atma*. Such people are fearless and cannot be manipulated.

Certain powerful lobbies, called the 'Deep State', who work behind the scenes to control humans world-wide, may not want that Vedic knowledge should become common knowledge, not even in Bharat. **They may not want humans to know that the Supreme Being is within them as loving, all-knowing Consciousness.**

But does the 'deep state' even know about the profundity of Indian Vedanta philosophy?

Yes, it does. The CIA, an important part of the 'deep state', declassified not only in 2003 the *Gateway Process Report*, which I have mentioned earlier, but also in 2016 a document on cultural trends study.[4]

It says:

> ...aside from this popular version of Hinduism, the religion has a sophisticated philosophical and ethical system, called Vedanta, based on the Upanishads section of the four Vedas.

So why is this 'sophisticated philosophical and ethical system' of Vedanta not studied and spread the world over for the benefit of humanity?

Instead, the Israeli historian, Yuval Noah Harari, a close associate of Klaus Schwab, former executive chairman of the World Economic Forum (WEF), declared belief in God and soul as ridiculous, and surely voiced the official line of those behind the *Great Reset* at the WEF, Bilderberg meetings, United Nations, and other such organisations. For them, man is God. Or rather, a few, ultra rich men see themselves as God, and capable of shaping the future of the world.

Harari said, '**Consciousness is not needed; intelligence is needed**'. And robots will be far more intelligent than humans. So, what did he mean?

---

4   Study on Cultural Trends: https://www.cia.gov/readingroom/print/1697631

He spelt it out:

'We will have many "useless people" who will have been replaced by intelligent robots.' And he suggested, that '**all the useless people, should be kept busy with computer games and drugs.**' Thankfully, he did not suggest (publicly at least) to kill them.

It means, they want to get us interested in gaming and '**living in a metaverse**', which means in Virtual Reality within this maya which itself, is not the 'real thing' but a misperception of our senses and mind. So, living in a metaverse would remove us one layer further from our divine roots, and leave us without meaning and purpose in life, without any anchor, without values. It would allow us to be easily controlled.

Isn't the disconnection from one's Inner Being or Atma already happening, especially in certain groups in the West, and also in India? Many have lost their connection with their conscience and deny the existence of God. The moral degradation has gone very far. For many, sensual enjoyment and riches have become the purpose of life.

Some have even sold their souls to Satan for fame and riches. Certain Hollywood actors, openly, on camera, have thanked Satan for their awards! And, the ultra-rich and powerful men (all men) have been found to perform dark rituals once a year, to a huge idol of an owl in the Bohemian Grove, an estate in the Redwoods of Northern California. (Alex Jones managed to infiltrate and secretly film it in the year 2000. He claims this ritual has been happening since 1873).

Surely, it is a paradox that the most benign, inclusive Hindu Dharma is singled out for eradication, and on the other hand, dark, occult rituals are practised by the topmost elite. This makes sense only, when this elite does NOT have the well-being of humanity (and neither the well-being of animals and nature) at heart. The chances are great that this is indeed the case.

India's wisdom about our divine essence (Atma) needs to be spread, quickly. Our identity is not one of numerous, fictitious genders. It is also not our person consisting of body and mind.

**Our identity is pure, blissful Consciousness.
This wisdom may just save humanity.**

Chapter 2

Basics of Vedic Wisdom

THERE ARE *many born Hindus who know much more about Vedic wisdom than I do, but sometimes it is easier for an outsider to see the most important aspects of the incredibly rich, incredibly vast Indian tradition. For me, this aspect is its profound philosophy that is expressed in the Upanishads.*

I would request you not to rush through this chapter. It needs a little patience. I have tried to put Advaita Vedanta (which is also close to Kashmir Shaivism) as simply and succinctly as I could. If you read about it for the first time, reflect on it in a quiet hour. It is helpful to have this knowledge as a base.

I was fortunate that soon after coming to Bharat, in 1980, at the Kumbh Mela in Haridwar, and in the presence of great gurus like Sri Anandamayi Ma and Devaraha Baba, I became familiar with this most important aspect. For Hindus, this may sound natural, but even they may not have reflected deeply on what this really means, because its implications are monumental.

Let me put it first in Western terminology:
God is within you!

By God, I mean that unfathomable, conscious power that is the cause of this universe, and NOT the God of the three Abrahamic religions (Judaism, Christianity, and Islam), who by definition is NOT within humans, but separate, somewhere in heaven.

Now, let me put it in Indian terminology:
You are one with Brahman—one with that invisible, blissful Consciousness. (*Sat-Chit-Ananda*).

Anandamayi Ma used to say:

'**There are no separate entities. All is one. Your senses deceive you. You are not a small person in a big world. In truth, there is nothing but Brahman or Ishwara and you are one with That.**'

Kena Upanishad, chapter 1, verse 5 says:

'What the mind does not comprehend, but because of which the mind comprehends, know THAT alone to be Brahman. Not this that people worship here.'

(यन्मनसा न मनुते येनाहुर्मनो मतम्।
तदेव ब्रह्म त्वं विद्धि नेदं यदिदमुपासते॥५॥)

Ramana Maharshi compared Brahman with the white screen on which a movie plays. The persons and things in the movie fully cover the screen and make it invisible, **yet the true substance of all those fleeting images is only the screen. It permeates all. If you try to touch any person in the movie, you will only touch the screen.**

Similarly, everything in this temporary universe is playing out on the eternal screen of Brahman. All is contained in Brahman and all is permeated by Brahman. There are no outside sources which project the images onto the screen, like in a movie hall. Here the screen itself (Brahman) manifests the images, thanks to its innate will-power (Maya-*Shakti*).

The four *Mahavakyas* (great sayings) of the Upanishads are the shortest expressions of the Absolute Truth:

Aham Brahmasmi (I am Brahman),
Tat Tvam Asi (That you are),
Pragyanam Brahma (Brahman is the highest knowledge),
Ayam Atma Brahma (This Atma is Brahman).

It means, the Consciousness in me (Atma) is one with the Universal Consciousness (Brahman). Everyone refers to himself as 'I'. This pure I, without name and form, is the same in everyone and it alone is *really* true. All else *seems* to be true, yet is a *temporary appearance* of *maya*, like the temporary movie on the permanent cinema screen.

Somehow, this immediately made sense to me. It tallies with what modern physics says: 'All is one energy'. When I learned 'All is one energy' for the first time in school, I thought, 'If there is a God, that must be it'. At that time, I had already some doubts about the Christian God. However, this insight felt abstract and theoretical, and I forgot about it.

It was only when I came to India, that I understood that Brahman is not something dead: **It is the living, loving Presence that is right here, right now.**

This highest philosophy is called Advaita Vedanta. It is based on three major ancient texts, namely the Upanishads, which are the last part of the Vedas, the Bhagavad Gita, and the *Brahma Sutra*.

Simply put:

Only Pure Consciousness (or pure awareness) is true

and eternal (like an infinite screen). This one, limitless Consciousness appears as many due to its innate divine power, called maya or shakti. The plurality does not exist independently. It has no substance by itself. It manifests temporarily within Brahman. One can also call it a dream of Brahman.

But how do we know that only Brahman is true?

The *Tripura Rahasya* mentions two conditions for Absolute Truth:
1. It must be always—past, present, future.
2. It must be self-evident—not needing anything else to be perceived.

The first condition already excludes the whole universe and the contents of consciousness, like thoughts and memories.

What fulfils the second condition?

Try to find out for yourself. Nothing that is perceived is the Absolute Truth, because it needs my Consciousness to be perceived.

The Truth is hidden in our own Consciousness. And it needs to be realised there.

Now, what is the point of all this? How does it affect us?

Let's think for a moment: What is most important in life? What is that without which, there is no point in existing at all?

What is the ONE thing that is absolutely essential?

Usually, we consider it so ordinary that we don't even take notice of it.

It is Consciousness.

Let me give an example. Suppose *Bhagawan* (God) appears to you and grants you whatever you wish. He does not put any limit to your wishes, only one condition: that you will not be conscious.

Can you see, how important Consciousness is? What is the point of all your wishes being fulfilled, if you are not aware? **Nobody will exchange billions of dollars for this ordinary thing of being conscious, isn't it?**

Yet, our ordinary consciousness mainly means thinking. Thoughts are the content or modification of 'Pure' Consciousness and are always changing.

Pure Consciousness means thought-free Consciousness which is unchanging.

Imagine, you shine a torch into a dark room. You see different things—chairs, tables, and other objects, but you don't notice the light. Or, you don't notice the space in the room that holds all those things…the light or the space is comparable with Pure Consciousness.

How will you discover or touch Pure Consciousness?

Yoga is the means to join us with THAT. It helps us in realising who we really are. And no, yoga is not only about *asanas*.

The first *shloka* of the Patanjali *Yoga Sutras* says:

Yoga is *Chitta Vritti Nirodh*—Yoga is about restraining thought waves.

Why is restraining thoughts so important? Because then the original, Pure Consciousness shines through.

Yogasara Upanishad says, 'Then there is communion with *Paramatma*'.

That is from where intuition comes, from where bliss comes, from where love comes.

Brahman is always present, beneath and between our thoughts, like the formless screen is always present beneath the different images of a movie.

Brahman or Paramatma or Ishwar (names don't matter for That—which is beyond words and thoughts) is within us.

It is the unchanging 'I AM' or rather, 'I KNOW THAT I AM', without any changing attributes like name, profession, or nationality.

Now, we also have the goal of human life:

If we live in a make-believe world, in maya, then to realise the Truth, is naturally the goal of life and its meaning and fulfilment.

For this, we need to do sadhana or spiritual practice. The Bhagavad Gita gives many helpful tips on *Jnana Yoga* (Yoga of knowledge), *Bhakti Yoga* (Yoga of devotion), and *Karma Yoga* (Yoga of action). A guru is also very helpful because only intellectual knowledge of what we really are is not enough.

Vedic knowledge needs to be lived.

Chapter 3

The Divine, Your Dearest Companion

WHAT ARE your suggestions for making Vedanta practical in one's daily life?

Basically, it is about sometimes stopping the thought stream and simply being in the Now. The mind prefers thoughts. It is not easy to stop them, especially nowadays, with so much information coming via the internet. Yet when you become aware that you are thinking, then you have the chance to stop it. Stop, at least for a few seconds. Feel the energy field inside the body or hear the sounds outside. Even this little awareness helps and may bring fresh ideas into the mind afterwards.

Another method, which I practised a lot in the beginning, is to remind myself that all this is just like a movie on Brahman's screen, in which Maria is an actor, but in reality, only the screen is real and solid. Similarly, in the depth of my being, I am one with Brahman....

Everyone must find a way of avoiding being sucked into thoughts and emotions so as to avoid drowning in these thoughts. The content of Consciousness is ever-changing. The Real Truth is unchanging. It is Sat-Chit-Ananda, blissful awareness.

Sometimes, while waking up in the morning, one gets a taste of this blissful, pure awareness. One is not asleep any longer, but has also not yet identified with one's person.

One of the texts of Kashmir Shaivism, *Vijnana Bhairava*, lists 112 methods on how to catch this state of pure awareness, which underlies our existence but gets covered with thoughts and emotions. For example, one of the methods is that after sneezing, when you get goosebumps, for that one tiny moment, pure awareness shines through. Try to catch it. Since we are not accustomed to it, we usually miss it.

One more thing that is helpful is being well-meaning towards all. And of course, being truthful.

How can we bring happiness into our daily life?

What I described in the previous answer is also the best way to bring happiness into our daily life. Yoga and pranayama are helpful. Feel the inner vibrations after yoga and pranayama. Don't run away with your thoughts and when you sit for meditation, resolve to stay focused on your mantra or whatever method you use, for at least fifteen minutes (or even 5), without trying to solve some problems in your head. Nevertheless, if you discover that you are still trying to solve problems, then stop as soon as you notice it.

India also has many helpful and joyful methods while being in the company of others. *Kirtan* or *bhajan* is a beautiful way of expressing one's devotion. Attending *Aarti* in a temple, going on a pilgrimage or listening to *kathas* or *satsang* is far more uplifting than strolling through a shopping mall.

Try to make the Divine your dearest companion; He is always with you; that's the best way to obtain happiness.

Repeating a mantra is a great help in keeping a loving connection to one's *Ishta Deva* (most beloved Deva).

Anandamayi Ma came from Advaita and kept stressing that 'All is one', yet at the same time, she put great stress on *Bhakti*, on love for Bhagawan. She used to say, 'Feel, you are in the loving embrace of Bhagawan. Always remember Him, twenty-four hours a day. Feel, He is living through you. When you walk, feel He is moving your legs. Always have His name on your lips….'

Once she asked a devotee why he constantly moved his mouth. 'Ma, you told me to always have something sweet on my tongue. So, I suck a toffee,' he replied. Ma laughed and clarified, 'By "something sweet" I meant the name of Hari. There is nothing sweeter than the name of your Ishta Deva. Keep it always on your tongue.'

But is there not a contradiction? When there is only one Brahman, where do the different Devas or Gods come from?

Well, the Devas (forces of light) are also part of this Maya, just like we humans are. Even the Devas are not eternal and independent of Brahman, though they live far longer and are far more powerful than humans. For example, according to the Puranas, a single day of the creator Brahma (not to confuse with the eternal Brahman) lasts for 4.32 billion human years.

Only in Maya there is duality of good and evil—it is not there in the *Nirgun* (formless) Brahman.

Therefore, within maya, there are also—apart from the 'good' Devas—the 'bad' Asuras (egoistic forces of darkness), against whom we need to guard ourselves. Anandamayi Ma assured us that negative, demonic forces have no power if we hold on to our Ishta Deva with the help of a mantra.

Anandamayi Ma would also say: 'Share freely what you have, whether it is knowledge or material things. If you do this, and also genuinely make Bhagawan the centre of your life, you will be taken care of.'

Strange as it may sound, especially to Western ears, fulfilling one's duty in one's station in life also gives happiness.

A practical, quick method of changing one's mood if one feels low is to dance with your arms up in the air. Try it out. It works. I learnt this in an Art of Living course. Or, sing loudly, for example the *Hanuman Chalisa*.

What are your views on getting enlightened?

In the beginning, my idea of being enlightened was very fuzzy. Somehow, I did not expect that it is possible for us 'normal' people to become enlightened. Yet the more I read and reflected, I realised that we all have the same potential, same as famous spiritual personalities.

And still later, after having meditated a lot, I felt enlightenment is basically a shift from the content of the mind towards pure awareness. When this happens, a very pleasant feeling of expansion comes with it, which is impossible to describe. Occasionally, I got a glimpse of it, but it's not in my hand to get into this state. It is granted only occasionally. Of course, my experience may be the lower rung on the ladder of enlightenment and many higher rungs are surely possible. But even this shift makes life extremely worthwhile.

Once Anandamayi Ma said: 'People feel pity for sanyasis because they have renounced the joys of the world. These people don't know what *they* are missing out on by being immersed only in worldly pleasures.'

Chapter 4

The Misunderstanding That Killed

THE TWITTER handle 'Hathyogi' once posted a thread on the 'Six major myths about Hinduism that needed to be debunked by every Hindu'. His first point was 'Hindus are idol-worshippers'.

I wrote the following comment:

'High time that Hindus debunk this false label of 'idol-worshippers' which is for Muslims and Christians the biggest sin and makes Hindus in their eyes the worst of creatures who are an offense to their 'true God'. This false label is a dangerous mark on them.'

Several Hindus reacted, 'We ARE idol-worshippers. Why should we care what others think?'

In this case, we should indeed care, especially since on a deeper level, Hindus see all as one, and are not worshipping 'other gods', which is the definition for idol-worship in the Abrahamic religions.

The problem is not with worshipping a representation of the Divine, called idol in English (the Catholic Church also uses idols), the problem lies with the extremely negative connotation which the Abrahamic religions have given to the term 'idol-worshipper' and of which most Hindus are not aware.

Most Hindus think that 'idol' is simply the translation of *pratima* or *murti*, but this is not the case. For Muslims and Christians, there is automatically a lot of hostile association when they hear this term, thanks to their indoctrination since childhood. I can speak only for Christians, but I am sure, it is the same or even more for Muslim children. This association comes not only with the English term, but also, for example, with the German term *Götzenanbeter*. It is a very bad label. It means a false god or false gods are worshipped. And, I have heard this in primary schools in connection with Hindus.

Worshipping idols is the greatest sin for Muslims, Christians, and Jews.

Hindus don't realise that. 'You shall not have other Gods before me' is the first commandment in Christianity and Judaism, and in Islam *shirk*, which means the same thing, is the worst evil a human can commit, and it will be severely punished with eternal hellfire. Members of the Abrahamic religions believe that only their God is the true God, and He has declared that ONLY HE must be worshipped, and others must not be considered 'before Him'. (Doesn't it imply that their god actually acknowledges that there are other gods?)

Still, it means that Hindus, who worship 'other' gods, are despicable for pious Muslims, Christians, and Jews. Hinduism is seen as going against the Will of God and, therefore, is seen as demonic or satanic. The followers of Abrahamic religions do not realise that their vengeful, biased God of the Old Testament is within maya, like the Devas and Asuras and everything else in this universe, and is not on the absolute level of Brahman.

Dehumanisation of Hindus
So, when Hindus say, 'What does it matter? Let them believe what they want,' they do not realise the danger. It DOES matter what the followers of Abrahamic religions believe. The consequences of their belief was that at least 80 million Hindus were killed simply for being Hindus over the centuries.

They were killed due to a misunderstanding or due to an intentional disinformation campaign that 'Hindus go against the Will of the only true God'.

And the killing still goes on, as the brutal terror attack in Pahalgam in Kashmir on 22 April 2025 sadly proved. The Muslim terrorists shot the men in front of their families after ascertaining that they were Hindus, and not circumcised. This could and can only happen, because Hindus were dehumanised and this continues.

The clergy, in tune with their religious texts, indoctrinate Muslim and Christian children to look down upon Hindus as sub-humans. Often the media, too, gives the impression that Hindus worship demons.

Hindus must take serious note of this unacceptable and highly dangerous vilification of Hindus, and urgently correct this wrong perception.

It startles me that Hindus do not set the record straight and attempt to make the followers of Abrahamic religions understand that Hinduism was the first tradition to postulate One Supreme Being, and Hindus are *not* idol-worshippers, in the sense that they do NOT worship different deities as *separate* entities.

All *Devas*, whom the Hindus worship, are in essence, only Brahman, the one Supreme Truth. However, within this diverse Maya, they manifest as different divine beings, as we humans manifest as different human beings.

The Abrahamic religions claim, 'There is only *one* God (separate from His creation)'. They don't know that the rishis claim that 'There is *only* God/Brahman (pervading and containing the universe)'.

If the clergy of the Abrahamic religions understood this, they would have absolutely no reason to accuse Hindus of going against the Will of their God. And they would have no reason to look down upon them. In fact, they might realise that the Hindu view is closer to Truth, as it worships the original One God from whom *everything* springs. Brahman is not a kind of tribal God, who looks after only a certain group of humans. Brahman is truly universal.

Hindu Dharma is about trying to connect with that inner essence which is witness to even our thoughts and feelings. It is about doing *sadhana* (including worshipping Devas and following dharma) and slowly becoming more familiar with that blissful awareness. Then, not only knowledge (*jnana*), but also love (bhakti) will develop.

Now, dear Muslim and Christian friends, do you feel that Hindus are despicable or rather, loveable?

Also, please reflect if the 'One true God' can possibly hate them for their faith and let them burn in hellfire under great agony for all eternity?

However, the denigration and 'othering' of Hindus continues in mainstream media. It indicates that big powers have an interest in degrading Hinduism as demonic.

In July 2022, the Canadian psychologist Jordan B Peterson

brought out a short video, where he exhorted Muslims to reach across the sectarian divide, to Shias, Sunnis, then to Christians, and to Jews. He advocated a unity of the 'people of the book' who 'have much in common'. And he added a rather sinister sentence, 'The best place to find Satan is within… the subtle temptation of the ancient demonic spirit'.

In seventeen hours, his video had one million views with every comment praising him.

Satan is within? Not Brahman/God? Maybe Peterson never looked deep enough to discover that thought-free Consciousness that gives us life, but saw only thoughts which tempt one to do wrong things?

Recently an Indian newspaper reported on a study that meditation (looking inward) can cause one to become mad!

Am I the only one who is sensing danger for Hindus from this dubious narrative?

Chapter 5

The Source of All is ONE

AT A seminar where Hinduism-related topics were being discussed, I asked some students during tea break, 'Can you explain what is the main aspect of Hinduism?'

There was an awkward silence. After a while, a girl said, 'Hindus worship many Gods.' I asked, 'Who created the many Gods?' Now the silence was permanent. Nobody ventured an answer.

'Did you ever hear of Brahman?' I asked. 'I do not mean Brahma, the creator God of the trinity Brahma, Vishnu, Shiva, but Brahman the Absolute Truth, the conscious Oneness behind this manifestation?'

No, none of them had heard of Brahman.

I could hardly believe it. How can the highest philosophy, discovered by the ancient rishis, and handed down through the Vedas, not be handed down to future Indian generations, when even German philosophers and scientists had praised it to the skies, when this knowledge had reached Europe a few hundred years ago?

Ever since, when I meet youngsters and there is a chance to have a conversation, I ask this question—'Can you explain what Hinduism is about?'

So far, nobody has told me about the basics of Bharat's ancient wisdom. It almost seems as if Indians are not supposed to know that their tradition has a higher, absolute level, above the relative multiplicity of this world. A level which is beyond thoughts and words, which is *A-dvaita*: not two, but ONE, and which makes the Indian tradition stand tall among traditions which came much later.

By making Indians forget about the highest teachings of their rishis, those later traditions give the impression that they, not the Indian tradition, have more reasonable explanations for the creation of the universe and are the more reasonable religions.

There cannot be many creators. It has to be One Supreme Power which is behind the plurality, and indeed, Christianity and Islam keep stressing the point that they worship One Creator-God, whereas Hindus worship many Gods, and, therefore, the monotheistic religions are the better choice and closer to the Truth. Both Christianity and Islam claim, that each alone is fully true.

They get away with it, because most Hindus don't know the profound insights of their rishis. Occasionally, Hindus argue with me on Twitter, 'Why should we conform with the Abrahamic religions? Let them worship one God. We have every right to worship many Gods. Don't tell us what we should do.'

Unfortunately, they misunderstand me.

Of course, nothing is wrong in worshipping many Gods. In fact, it makes great sense.

There is an incredible variety in this world, so there are naturally different 'departments' to be looked after by different deities. If you have some problem, you approach the head of the specific department—and so you can ask Saraswati Devi for wisdom, Lakshmi Devi for wealth, Sri Ganesh to remove obstacles, Shiva or Vishnu for spiritual upliftment and so on.

But if Hindus don't know that these different deities are ultimately One with the One Brahman, they basically concede that those two religions are more reasonable, which they are not.

The source of all must be One, and is One.

Chapter 6

Drawbacks of Hinduism

WHAT ARE the drawbacks of Hinduism apart from idol-worship? This was a question on Quora to which I replied, thus:

Why do you write 'apart from idol worship'? Too much Christian brainwashing that idols are just stones? Hindus consider the whole universe alive, as ultimately Brahman. Nothing wrong in taking the help of a 'form', a *murti*, to feel closer to the Divine by worshipping it.

Coming back to the original question: There are no drawbacks in Hindu Dharma, since it is a genuine, outer and inner enquiry into what is true about us and the universe and helpful for a fulfilling life. The truth is non-negotiable, but rules for society are flexible. In the last chapter of *Manu Smriti* for example, it is mentioned that the rules can be changed by a group of either three or even one knowledgeable Brahmin according to the times. (*Manu Smriti* XII. 112/113)

However, since the last 2,000 years, dogmatic religions have appeared on the scene which make unsubstantiated claims about 'Truth', and are highly aggressive in trying to get the whole world to believe what they claim as truth. Hinduism proved to be too generous and good-natured. It did not suspect that people could cheat others in the name of truth. Its tenet 'Truth is one, the wise call it by many names' is applicable only to 'well meaning' claims about truth, and not to incredible dogmas which are meant to frighten people of eternal hell and to gain worldly power.

Unfortunately, British education weaned Indians away from knowing what their tradition is, by not letting them know their Sanskrit scriptures. So, drawbacks are with Indians: first, many wrongly believe that Hinduism is inferior, due to the British brainwashing, and second, even if they realise that it is not so, they find it hard to explain the advantages of Hinduism, as they know too little, and fall easy prey to a Western lifestyle (which obviously is a failed model) or even for Western religions which tend to produce hypocrites.

As an afterthought, it occurred to me that Hindu Dharma has indeed a serious drawback: If the rishis, after compiling their profound insights in the Vedas, would have added one sentence—just one sentence—it would have made a big difference. If they had added, 'Whoever does not believe in the Vedas and Veda Vyasa, will burn eternally in hellfire,' then Hinduism would also be one of the respected religions like Christianity and Islam.

Of course, this is sarcasm and not meant to be taken seriously. But it may give food for thought of how irrational the debate on religion has become in the last 2,000 years.

Chapter 7

Indian Wisdom and Modern Science

IN FEBRUARY 1982, I was asked by a German magazine to cover a conference in Mumbai at the Oberoi Sheraton on the 'Convergence of Ancient Wisdom and Modern Science'. There, for the first time, I understood that science indeed claims that there are no separate objects, but that All is one—in tune with India's ancient wisdom.

At that time, I thought that now, finally, Advaita Vedanta would become common knowledge—but I was wrong. The following article was written thirty years later, and mainstream science still considers it a fringe theory that this one energy is conscious, as Vedanta claims. Western science ignores it completely (and hopes that people have forgotten) that earlier great scientists such as Max Planck or Erwin Schrödinger, had endorsed the Indian view.

Are we not supposed to know that this amazing, miraculous energy within us is AWARE and ALIVE?

Modern science has come to the conclusion that all is one energy. Long ago, India's wisdom had come to the conclusion that all is one awareness/consciousness, i.e. the one energy of science 'knows itself'. It is not inert, not dead, but alive with consciousness. So far, science either does not know about the claim of the Indian rishis, which is highly unlikely, or fights shy of investigating it.

Suppose there is a scientist whose theories have always turned out to be right. Now, this scientist comes up with yet another theory that is different from the theories that the rest of the scientific community holds. And, however hard these scientists have tried, they could not prove their own theory. Would it not be worthwhile, to test the theory of that one scientist who so far has had an amazing success rate?

Well, this scientist refers to the rishis of ancient India. Most Western scientists haven't ever heard of these rishis. They don't know what they had postulated and it may also not interest them as science has made amazing progress in the last century and theories that were several thousand years old have no role to play today. Or have they a role to play?

Most scientists are engaged in tedious work in their labs. Their field of research is highly specialised and path-breaking technology has emerged from it. Yet, there are also scientists who look at an big picture, who, like Einstein or Hawking, want to find an explanation for everything in this universe, a unified theory, also called a 'theory of everything'. They try to push the frontiers of knowledge to reach the Absolute Truth. But it has eluded them so far.

Maybe they should turn to the Indian rishis for inspiration. Certainly, their track record is amazing. Thousands of years ago, these rishis had claimed that the age of our present (according to them it is not the first) universe is mind boggling, whereas the West maintained till a few hundred years ago, that it was created some 6,000 years back.

The rishis knew that there are many suns, that atoms make up matter, and at the same time, that the whole universe is one, that this world is maya, an appearance or superimposition on that what is really true. It is similar to a cup that is a superimposition on mud or a bangle on gold—the cup and the bangle are only relatively or temporarily true, whereas the mud and the gold are the true essence.

The rishis even knew that the best symbol for the Whole is a *Lingam*. Is it surprising that the 'big picture of the entire Universe' which was released by the Max Planck Institute has an oval shape?

All this and much more has turned out to be correct, even though some insights, for example 'the world is maya' had actually been ridiculed in the West, till modern physics, too, came to the conclusion that nothing is as it appears. Science has reached a point where ultimately nothing can be said with certainty, where, so to speak, matter contains no matter!

In our perception, an apple is still an apple and still falls to the ground. Yet, if one enquires into what an apple truly is, one ends up with nothing in one's hand. Not even the hand is there as a hand. In short: the senses deceive. Truth is something else.

This is the point where ancient India could help science in making a decisive step or rather, a decisive turnaround towards finding the truth. Nuclear physics has come to the conclusion that 'All is one energy'. This insight was hailed at an international conference over 40 years ago as coming together of 'Ancient wisdom and modern science'.

India's wisdom says: All is one and modern science, too, says: All is one.

Yet, there is still a big difference and it may be frustrating for the few scientists who are ready to bridge this gap, but the scientific community, as a whole, is opposed to it.

The difference is: Rishis claim that this one energy is aware or conscious of itself.

Awareness means knowing, being alive. Whatever seems to exist, comes out of one, absolute Awareness. It follows that the universe is alive. There is a Presence in it, and this one Presence appears as many and expresses itself through the human brain. The brain can be seen as an adequate instrument to manifest pure, thought-free Awareness as thoughts, feelings, memories, imagination, etc., like a light bulb manifests electricity as light. The light bulb does not generate electricity, nor does the brain generate awareness.

Here, mainstream science refuses to go along. It holds that the energy that makes up our universe is 'dead'. It does not know itself. Yet, there is also the obvious fact that humans on earth are aware, and mainstream science still considers this awareness as being produced by the brain, even though it can't prove it. According to modern science, consciousness developed accidentally as a by-product of the chemical activity in our inert brain cells.

If one manipulates these brain cells, the human mind undergoes changes. This fact is considered a vindication of their theory. Yet, does the light not look red, if one paints the bulb red? The output changes if the equipment is manipulated, but the input, the electricity, is the same.

Science further holds that conditions have to be agreeable for this awareness by-product to happen and these favourable conditions are extremely rare. But on our earth, life and awareness had a chance to develop from matter. These conditions may also be present in some other planets in space. Otherwise, the universe is inert, dead, and chance and time are ruling it.

There is no knowledge of what is happening in the cosmos apart from those few exceptions, like on our earth. As a natural consequence of this theory, human awareness dies when the brain dies—like a flicker of light that dies with the firefly. Awareness does not find a place in equations that try to explain cosmic laws.

There may be two reasons why Western scientists avoid giving place to Awareness.

One is that in the West, the Church has been the sole keeper of the 'Truth' and has severely crippled scientific ventures for over a thousand years. Only a few hundred years ago and with great difficulty, men of courage overcame the oppressive stranglehold of the Church. Ever since, science not only ignores religion, but is opposed to it because, in the West, 'religion' promotes as the 'Highest Truth', a personal God, who watches over all humans and loves some and hates others. Of course, this is anathema to scientists. They are out to prove almost with a vengeance, that there is no God, and terms like Awareness or Consciousness may bring in God through the back door.

There is another reason why scientists overlook awareness, even though, if they would only look, it stares them in the face or rather, out from their face.

Awareness cannot be objectified, because it is the subject.

Traditionally, science is focussed on objects, i.e. on the observed. Only lately, it has included the observer, after it became evident that the observer influences the observed. Yet, basically, it treats the observer as just another object. The scientist does not dive into his own living awareness to find out about the observer, but places the 'observing system' in one line with the objects under observation. He does not realise that his subjective, living awareness is a completely different category and requires an inner exploration.

For anyone who is interested in finding the truth, and scientists supposedly are, the most obvious and crucial factor in any research, the living Consciousness (that can be felt by anyone and without which there would be no scientific research at all), surely cannot be dismissed with the improvable assumption that it is a sort of secretion or 'epiphenomenon' of the inert brain. That would be unscientific, more so, since there is ample literature on Awareness/Consciousness in India.

This literature gives us valuable clues. For example, the scriptures have two major terms—*Atman* and Brahman. Atman (also called Atma) refers to the seemingly individualised awareness (often translated as 'Self') and Brahman to the infinite, Absolute Awareness. The scriptures claim that Brahman cannot be spoken or thought of. It has no attributes. Brahman is that by which the thoughts and speech are made possible. It is the independent, Absolute Truth that eludes objectification, as it is one subject. Brahman alone is the Truth, the Vedas declare.

Now if we look at Atman, we are on more familiar ground. It is the capacity to know and feel and this capacity is within all of us. It is what makes us feel alive. The scriptures have analysed our inner composition in great detail. There are efforts to compile this knowledge into textbooks and teach it in psychology courses at the university level.

Let us return to the big picture.

There are intriguing statements in the Vedas. They are called *Mahavakyas*, the great utterances. These statements claim that 'This Atma is Brahman' or 'You are That'. It means that our own, individual awareness or self is one with the great, all-pervading Brahman. It further means that the great One Brahman is right here.

How can that be? Is our human awareness not rather ordinary?

It is my direct experience that I am Maria, and certainly not Brahman? On the other hand, it is also my direct experience that the world is real, but it has been proven to be illusory. Could this feeling that I am Maria also be illusionary?

'Who am I?' is the big and ultimate question in Indian philosophy.

Its answer may throw up the unified theory and what is more worthwhile, fulfilment. Yet the answer cannot be put into words and neither into research papers. Scientists need to turn around and dive deep within themselves, beyond their thoughts and feelings, right down to the pure, thoughtless Awareness.

Indian scriptures offer another approach.

According to them, everything in the Universe has five components. The first two—name and form—keep changing. They belong to the world of maya. Beneath these two, there is Sat-Chit-Ananda: Sat = being, Chit = awareness, Ananda = bliss. Basically, these three are one and unchanging.

Science takes note only of name and form, and of *Sat* (being). Something is there. Yet *Chit*, the awareness and *Ananda*, the bliss that comes with awareness, are missing.

Modern science presents us with a rather bleak scenario, where basically, there is no meaning in living, all is chance and everything finishes with the death of the body. But, it is still the in-thing to believe among the so-called intellectuals of the West.

The bleakness is not due to the fact that science considers the human mind a temporary flicker. Even the Indian rishis consider the mind as thoughts, modifications in pure awareness that are ultimately as unreal as the solidity in matter.

The bleakness is rather due to the fact that scientists don't figure in the big (the word Brahman comes from big, expanding) living, blissful Presence, Intelligence, Awareness, Absolute or whatever name we want to give to the Divine.

The rishis claim that it is here, right beneath the individual awareness of thoughts. Thoughts prevent the experience of the underlying pure awareness, like ripples in water prevent one from seeing the river or sea bed. Rishis encourage the stilling of thoughts with the help of meditation. When thoughts are stilled, it becomes obvious that there is no separate individual awareness.

There is only Brahman.

In all likelihood, the rishis have deeper insights. The *Chandogya Upanishad* describes how Sage Uddalaka prodded his son Svetaketu to know 'That by knowing which everything is known', and how he helped his son with valuable questions and metaphors. Today, scientists also search for 'That by knowing which everything is known', but they still have a blind spot. They don't search where it is to be found—within their own awareness.

Eventually, they may realise that the rishis were right, but before this happens, they will have to learn to 'look' or rather 'sink' inside. Then, sacredness and wonder might overwhelm them: What a miracle! I am and know that I am—spread out all over, immortal!

Chapter 8

If Westerners Knew Facts about Hinduism

IN APRIL 2024, two big American influencers, Russell Brand and Candace Owens, declared that they were baptised. Others, who are already Christian like Tucker Carlson, keep stressing the importance of Christianity for a healthy society. Jordan Peterson explained why atheism is irrational. And of course, he has a point. There MUST be a great power behind this miraculous, vast universe. It couldn't have happened by chance. More and more Westerners are going back to their childhood belief that this great power is the Christian God or Jesus.

Even though I criticise Christianity, I consider that for normal Westerners (not clerics) it is more preferable to believe in Jesus and God, the Father than to be rootless atheists or communists, as long as they don't buy into the dogma of the Church that 'only Christianity can save you' and despise Hindus for their faith.

If this single dogma ('only the Church can save you') was

given up, Christianity could be like a branch of Hinduism focused on devotion for Jesus. But will the Vatican ever do so? Probably not, because its worldly power and wealth would decline, and worldly power seems to be its foremost endeavour, not spiritual truth.

Generally, Hindus living abroad do not discuss their faith, and have allowed the Church, academia, media, and even movies to shape a negative view of Hinduism. But even in Bharat, many Hindus don't articulate, and maybe don't know, the essence of the tradition which they have inherited.

Before the 2024 India elections, I watched a documentary on India on German TV. It was heavily biased against Prime Minister Narendra Modi and Hindus. Yet there was an incident, where a diamond businessman in Gujarat could have easily corrected the view of Hinduism for the German viewers:

'What is special about India?' the businessman was asked.

His reply: 'We believe in God, get our strength from Him, and start our day with a common prayer.'

'Which God? You have so many,' the German interviewer continued.

'Yes, we have many gods. I, personally, pray to Swami Narayana.' He then turned to someone standing nearby, and asked, 'To whom do you pray?'

If only he had mentioned that the different gods are aspects of the one all-pervading Brahman, Hinduism would have looked very different to German viewers and closer to the Truth as well.

I recently tweeted: *'A pity that Vedic knowledge/Hinduism is not known in the West. It is the best option for humanity. Sadly, certain forces don't want people to know that.'*

A foreigner reacted to my tweet:

'Excuse me, but yoking yourself to Hindu DEMON GODS is NOT the best path for humanity.' The capital letters were his.

This tweeter has obviously fallen prey to the mischievous propaganda he hears all the time.

It reminded me of the World Hindu Congress in Bangkok in November 2023. I was asked to talk on 'Articulating Hindu Thoughts', because this is an area where Hindus don't always do a good job.

For example, there are several videos on the net, where Shiva is compared to Satan—not by missionaries but by Westerners who talk positively about the Gods of ancient Egypt or Mesopotamia, even if those 'Gods' demanded child sacrifice and were truly demonic. Usually, India's ancient tradition is not mentioned at all, and if it is mentioned, it is done so in a negative way.

So, the comment about the Hindu demon gods didn't surprise me, but pained me nevertheless. Can Hindus do a better job of communicating what Hinduism is about?

I remembered my notes from the World Hindu Congress:

First: we need to clearly articulate what is most essential in the Vedic tradition. It is:

Brahman alone is true (= Absolute Truth). The world is an appearance in Brahman (= relative truth).

The world is dependent on Brahman and is temporary. Here 'the world' includes not only the visible Universe, including humans, but also the much maligned "many Hindu Gods". They also depend on the one Brahman for their existence, just as humans do.

Brahman is pure, thought-free Consciousness. It is the substratum on which thoughts and things appear. Thoughts are also objects. I can observe 'my' thoughts. So, who am I?

This is the most important question.

'Aham Brahmasmi' (I am Brahman) or *'Ayam Atma Brahma'* (this Atma is Brahman) claim the Vedas. We need sadhana to wear down the veil that hides our innermost Self.

So, is there any doubt that 'God', as the West calls the highest Truth, is within us? Are we not conscious, even though we are usually conscious only of 'objects' (thoughts) that are within our pure, conscious essence?

To discover thought-free Consciousness is the meaning of life. It is very close to us. So close that any closer is not possible because it is our Self. It is the Self in all.

Some Christian and Muslim mystics also discovered their oneness with That which alone truly is—probably thanks to intense bhakti (devotion).

Mansur Al-Hallaj, the ninth-century Persian mystic and poet openly declared, 'An *al-Haq*' (I am the Truth), and was killed for it. Meister Eckhart, the German theologian was outed from the Church for experiencing and teaching Oneness.

In Bharat, such persons are venerated.

Does this make sense so far? Does it not sound like highest philosophy?

Two hundred years ago, and even until 40 years ago, it also made sense to people in the West, to philosophers, to scientists, and to many hippies. Yet today, this profound knowledge has been blacked out. If you Google 'The greatest philosophers of all times', not a single Indian is mentioned among the fifty listed, while ancient Greeks, Chinese, and Arabs are mentioned.

WHY?

This is surely intriguing.

Unfortunately, even modern Indians have forgotten this

basic knowledge, and Hindus who knew, didn't do a good job of communicating their knowledge.

A few years ago, seventy years after the British left, I had attended an Interfaith Dialogue and was shocked that the Hindu side didn't ask a single straight question to the representatives of the Abrahamic religions and did not mention the positive sides of Hindu Dharma.

'I can't afford to be controversial. I have a family,' a participant said afterwards to me to explain his timidity. This is very unfortunate, because not putting things straight and making them understand can become very costly for Hindus in future. The past may repeat itself, if we have not learnt from it. And it already keeps repeating itself in the gruesome violence against Hindus in Bangladesh in 2024 or in Pahalgam in April 2025 where Hindu men on vacation with their families were mercilessly shot dead, merely because they were Hindus.

Whenever Hindus are victims, the world media hardly takes notice or makes it even look as if Hindus are to blame. There seems to be a directive from above to play down hate crimes against Hindus. Media has enormous powers. It can make those crimes disappear. And it can even turn good people into villains.

Fortunately, in our times, less people trust mainstream media—as they have pushed false narratives far too often, and for too long.

Chapter 9

When Germany is Christian, is India Hindu?

THE FOLLOWING article was very popular. It also went viral on WhatsApp. Its popularity provoked V Raghunathan, an NRI from Canada with a long, impressive bio, to write a counter under the rubric 'Outraged' as a Times of India blog in January 2020. He titled it: 'Why Maria Wirth is wrong?' which showed right on top for several years whenever one Googled my name. Here it is. Decide for yourself if I am wrong.

Though I have lived in India for a long time, there are still issues here that I find hard to understand. For example, why do so many educated Indians become agitated when India is referred to as a Hindu country? Majority of the Indians are Hindus. India is special because of its ancient Hindu tradition. Westerners are drawn to India because of Hinduism. Then, why is there resistance by many Indians to acknowledge the Hindu roots of their country? Why do some people give the impression that an India which valued those roots would be dangerous? Don't they know better?

This attitude is strange for two reasons.

First, those educated Indians have a problem only with 'Hindu' India, but not with 'Muslim' or 'Christian' countries. For example, Germany is a secular country, and only 49 per cent of the population is registered with the two big Christian churches (Protestant and Catholic). Nevertheless, the country is bracketed under 'Christian countries' and no one objects to it.

Angela Merkel, as Chancellor, had stressed the 'Christian roots of Germany' and had urged the population 'to go back to Christian values'. In 2012, she even postponed her trip to the G-8 Summit to make a public address on 'Catholics Day'. Two major German political parties carry 'Christian' in their names, including Angela Merkel's Christian Democratic Union.

Germans are not incensed that Germany is called a Christian country, though I would actually understand if they were. After all, the history of the Church is appalling.

The so-called success story of Christianity depended greatly on tyranny.

'Convert or die' were the options given—only some five hundred years ago to the indigenous population in South America, but also 1,200 years ago in Germany, when Emperor Karl the Great ordered the death sentence for refusal of baptism in his newly conquered realms. This provoked his advisor Alkuin to comment: 'One can force them for baptism, but how to force them to believe?'

Thankfully, those times, when one's life was in danger for dissenting with the dogmas of Christianity are over. Today, many in the West dissent and are leaving the Church in a steady stream. They are disgusted with the unholy behaviour of certain Church officials, and they also can't believe in the dogmas. For example, that 'Jesus is the only way' and that

God sends those who don't accept this claim, eternally to hell.

The second reason why I can't understand the resistance to associate India with Hinduism is:

Hinduism is in a completely different category from the Abrahamic religions.

Its history, compared to Christianity and Islam, was undoubtedly by far the least violent as it spread in ancient times by convincing arguments and not by force.

Hinduism is not a belief-system that demands blind acceptance of the dogmas and suspension of one's intelligence. On the contrary, it encourages one to use intelligence to the hilt. It is an enquiry into truth, based on refined character and intellect. It comprises a huge body of ancient literature, not only on dharma and philosophy, but also on mathematics, architecture, music, dance, science, astronomy, economics, politics, and other such subjects.

If Germany or any other Western country had this kind of literary treasures, they would be proud and highlight its greatness on every occasion.

For example, when I discovered the Upanishads, I was stunned. Here, it was expressed in clear terms what I had intuitively felt to be true, but could not have expressed clearly: Brahman is not partial; it is the invisible, indivisible, Conscious Essence in everything. Everyone gets a chance again and again, in life after life, to discover the Ultimate Truth and is free to choose his way back to it. Helpful hints are given but never imposed.

In my early years in India, I thought all Indians knew and valued their traditions. Slowly, I realised that I was wrong.

The British colonial masters had been successful in not only weaning away many of the elite from their ancient

tradition, but even making them despise it.

It helped that the British-educated class could no longer read the original Sanskrit texts and believed what the Britishers had told them.

This lack of knowledge and the brainwashing by the British education system may be the reason why many so-called 'modern' Indians are against anything Hindu. They don't realise the difference between Western religions that have to be believed blindly, and which discourage, if not forbid, their adherents to think on their own, and the multi-layered Hindu Dharma which gives freedom and encourages one to use their intelligence.

Many of India's educated classes do not realise that those who dream of imposing Christianity or Islam on this vast country will applaud them for denigrating the Hindu Dharma, because this creates a vacuum where Western ideas can easily gain a foothold.

At the same time, many Westerners, including staunch Christians, know the value of Hindu culture and surreptitiously appropriate insights from the vast Indian knowledge system, drop the original Hindu source and present it either as their own or make it look as if these insights had already been known in the West.

As the West appropriates valuable and exclusive Hindu assets, what it leaves behind is deemed inferior. Unwittingly, these 'modern' Indians are helping what Rajiv Malhotra of Infinity Foundation has called the Digestion of Dharma civilisation into Western universalism. That, which is being digested, a deer for example (analogue to Hindu Dharma), disappears whereas the tiger (analogue to Western Universalism) becomes stronger.

If only missionaries denigrated Hindu Dharma, it would not be so bad, as they clearly have an agenda which discerning Indians would detect. But sadly, Indians with Hindu names assist them because they wrongly believe that Hinduism is inferior to the Western religions. They belittle everything Hindu instead of getting in-depth knowledge about it. As a rule, they know little about their tradition except what the British have deceptively taught them, i.e., that the major features are the caste system and idol worship. They don't realise that India would gain, not lose, if it solidly backed its profound and all-inclusive Hindu tradition.

The Dalai Lama said that, as a youth in Lhasa, he had been deeply impressed by the richness of Indian thought. 'India has great potential to help the world,' he added.

Will the Westernised Indian elite realise this?

Chapter 10

Is Hindu Dharma Good, and Hindutva Bad?

'WHEN GERMANY is Christian, is India Hindu?' (see chapter 9) got amazingly good responses with thousands of Facebook likes. However, some readers felt that I had made a mistake by not distinguishing between good, tolerant Hinduism, which is a private belief, and bad, intolerant Hindutva, which, they claimed, stands for the 'communal agenda of an extreme right Hindu party that wants to force uniform Hinduism on this vast country, an act which is completely un-Hindu and against the pluralism of India'.

Is *Hindutva* (-*tva* is a suffix which means -ness, like Hindu-ness) really different from Hindu Dharma and is it dangerous? Or have those, who coined the term, an interest in making it look like that? No doubt, Hindutva has a bad name in the eyes of many, in spite of the Supreme Court ruling in 1995:

'Hindutva is indicative more of the way of life of the Indian people. ...Considering Hindutva as hostile, inimical, or intolerant of other faiths, or as communal proceeds from an improper appreciation of its true meaning.'

I would like to explain from a personal angle why I came to the conclusion that it is indeed 'an improper appreciation of its true meaning', when Hindutva is branded as communal and dangerous.

For many years, I lived in 'spiritual India' without any idea of how important the terms 'secular' and 'communal' were. The people I met were appreciative of India's great heritage. They gave me tips on which texts to read, which sadhus and gurus to meet, which mantras to learn, etc., and I wrote about India's wisdom and tradition mainly for the readers of the German magazine *Esotera*, to which I contributed till 2001.

I used to think that all Indians are genuinely proud of their ancestors, who had stunningly deep insights into what is true about us and the universe, and who had left a huge legacy of precious ancient texts that were unparalleled in the world.

Yet in 2002, when I settled in a 'normal' environment away from the ashrams and pilgrimage places and connected with the English-speaking middle class, including some of whom had foreign wives, I was shocked that several of my new Hindu friends were ridiculing Hindu Dharma without knowing anything about it. They had not even read the Bhagavad Gita, but pronounced severe judgment on Hinduism. They gave the impression as if Hinduism was the most depraved and violent of all religions and responsible for all the ills that India was facing. The caste system and crude rules of *Manu Smriti* were quoted as proof. Reading newspapers and watching TV, I also discovered an inexplicable, yet clear anti-Hindu stand.

My new acquaintances expected me to join them in denouncing 'primitive' Hinduism which I could not do, as I knew too much, not only from reading extensively, but also from doing sadhana. They were not amused and declared that

I had read the wrong books! They asked me to read the right books, which would give me the 'correct' understanding. They did not doubt their own view to be the correct one.

However, instead of coming around by reading Romila Thapar's books and similar treatises, I got the impression that there was an intention behind the wrong negative portrayal of Hinduism: Christianity and Islam were meant to look good in comparison.

My neighbour, at that time, was a writer with communist leanings. Henceforth, he introduced me to his friends with the words—'She is the local RSS *pracharak*'. Many 'secular' Indians consider the RSS as an organisation of Hindu fundamentalists, occasionally even equating it with Islamic terror groups. So, no surprise, that an elderly lady once retorted, 'In this case, I am not pleased to meet you.'

What was my 'fault'? I had dared to say that I love Hindu Dharma, as it (its off-springs Buddhism, Jainism, and Sikhism come close) is the only religion that is inclusive and not divisive, whereas Christianity and Islam divide humanity into those who have the 'True Faith', and those who are wrong and will pay for it eternally in hell, if not already on earth.

Standing up for Hindu Dharma (and not only following it in private) indicted me as belonging to the 'Hindutva brigade' that is shunned by Leftists and mainstream media. Of course, my stand was neither communal nor dangerous for India.

Hindu Dharma is indeed inclusive with a profound philosophy, and needs to gain strength at the expense of the Abrahamic religions, which are excluding 'others' and therefore, are communal.

Chapter 11

Letter on Hinduism vs. Hindutva

IT IS becoming a fashion to declare Hindutva as bad and Hinduism as good, mostly by people who don't know from their own experiences what it means to be a Hindu, like recently, Rahul Gandhi and Salman Khurshid.

Some time ago, there was an article in the 'Garhwal Post' by Dr Satish C Aikant, who agreed with Salman Khurshid that 'denouncing Hindutva for its deviation from Sanatan Dharma, is indeed making a case for Hinduism.'

I wrote a reader's letter to 'Garhwal Post':

Sir,

This refers to your article 'Quibbling over Hinduism and Hindutva' dated 12.12.21

The author wrote, 'It can be categorically stated that Hinduism and *Hindutva* are distinct and oppositional in nature. The distinction is, however, academic and cannot be appreciated by the common man.'

Isn't this a bit arrogant towards the 'common man'? Is this distinction not rather an academic and not very honest hair-splitting? *Hindutva* is the Indian word for what the British called Hinduism.

Yet it is true, that Hindutva denotes nowadays a more outspoken Hinduism. Do you remember the early days of the internet, when the so-called 'internet Hindu' was attacked for standing up for Hinduism? Now, instead of the 'internet Hindu', it's called Hindutva, and certain sections of society are not comfortable with the fact that the 'meek Hindu' has found out that his tradition is actually not as bad as it was made to be by the colonial powers, and that in fact, it is superior.

Now when I say 'superior', those who are attacking Hindutva as bigoted and dangerous, may feel vindicated, 'Look, *Hindutvadis* are supremacists. They need to be stopped. They will persecute those of other religions.'

Do those persons even know what Christianity and Islam claim?

These two religions do not postulate that they are superior but they assert that they are '*only true*' and that all those who don't accept this, will burn in hell forever.

The claim of being superior is open for enquiry and debate.

Daily during shopping, we need to choose between superior and inferior qualities and choose the superior one.

Yet 'only true' is different. It is not open for enquiry or debate.

It is an absolute claim which, however, is not backed up by any evidence. It is based only on the words of the founder of the religion, which has to be believed blindly (and which was written down sometimes centuries after he allegedly said it).

Here, the academics should come in and sort out the reasons why 'religion' has become so intolerant and violent, and has cost millions of lives ever since 'the Only True' religions appeared on the scene.

Hindus have been the victims for over a thousand years. They still are, just look at the fate of Hindus at the hands of Muslims in Pakistan or Bangladesh or even in India.

What hinders academics from looking at religions and their doctrines honestly?

Hinduism or Hindutva is interested in genuine spiritual upliftment.

Can this be said about the 'only true' religions??

Yet these religions have one great advantage: they have many apologists whose dishonest views are inexplicably amplified by mainstream and social media.

Yours,
Maria Wirth

Chapter 12

Is Hinduism a Religion or a Way of Life?

IT IS often said that Hinduism is not a religion, but a way of life. Or, is it a religion?

What is true?

It depends on how religion is defined.

Unfortunately, there is no clear-cut definition of religion. But most people probably would say that religion is:
- About believing in an invisible Supreme Being, which is the cause of our existence
- About methods and rituals of worship
- About living according to its laws or will

In this case, Hinduism is definitely a religion. In fact, it is the mother of all religions, because the Indian Vedas had already postulated in very ancient times the existence of such a Supreme Being. They called it Brahman (from big) or Paramatma or Parama Shiva or simply Tat (That) and had declared that it cannot be imagined by the human mind. Nevertheless, a kind of description is given: Sat-Chit-

Ananda (which means, Truth, Knowledge, and Bliss). It is all-pervading and, therefore, the essence (Latin: *esse* = to be) of everything, including us.

So why does the question arise whether Hinduism is a religion?

To discover this, we need to look at those religions where nobody has a doubt that they are religions. The term 'religion' was first used for the Catholic Church and later for Islam, too, and nobody has a doubt that Christianity and Islam are the main religions in today's world.

These two religions are also about the three points I have mentioned earlier in the chapter. Yet there are significant differences.

The Supreme Being (called God or Allah respectively) of these two religions is not the essence in all, but is a separate entity which has certain personal traits. One most important trait is that it is jealous of other Gods and wants the whole of humanity to worship only Him (yes, the Supreme is clearly imagined as a male). Both religions give out a dire warning: those who do not accept this truth will burn eternally in hell.

How do these religions know that this is the truth? Because they claim that the Supreme Being Himself has revealed this truth to one person (in the case of Christianity to Jesus Christ some 2,000 years ago and in the case of Islam, to Prophet Mohammed some 1,400 years ago).

Here is where another definition of religion comes in. It is often said that religion is a 'belief-system'. It needs blind, unverifiable belief in what the 'founder' of the religion has said and which has been written down in a book.

Here Hinduism is clearly not a religion. Hinduism does not require blind belief. On the contrary, it is an open enquiry and an inner exploration into the truth, especially into the truth of one's own being. It is necessary to discover the Divine Essence in oneself; to discover that *Atman* (one's Consciousness) is indeed Brahman, as the Vedas proclaim.

So, does it mean that Hinduism is not a religion?

Let's look at the word meaning of religion. *Religare* (Latin) means 'to bind back'. Bind to whom or to what?

Does it mean to bind the human to the Supreme Being or does it mean to bind to the doctrine taught by that religion?

If we look at history, the Church (for which the term 'religion' was first used) was very adamant that the followers which it had gained through (mostly forced) baptism must never leave the Church. Christianity had strict blasphemy laws with terrible punishments, like Islam has even today. So, it can be safely assumed that religion meant to bind its followers to the doctrine of that respective religion. The followers must 'religiously' stick to the doctrine.

If it would have meant to be bound to the Supreme Being, then surely Christianity or Islam should have no objection if the Supreme is called by another name, for example Shiva, and the process of being bound to Him is known as 'Yoga'.

So, in this sense, Hinduism is not a religion.

But it is also not just a way of life. It has many rules on how to live life in an ideal way. One could, therefore, say, Hinduism is an ideal, dharmic way of life which is helpful in realising one's ONENESS with the Supreme Being.

This ideal way of life is not based on a dogmatic belief system, but on dharma—experiential wisdom about what is the right thing to do in a given situation.

However, there is one important caveat:

Since 'religions' are legally and socially greatly privileged in today's world, it would be a blunder to leave the field of 'religion' to Christianity and Islam. Those two religions would triumphantly wade into that vacuum and might try even more forcefully than at present, to convert Hindus. They might claim (and they are experts in unsubstantiated claims) that everyone has a right to religion. Therefore, since Hindus don't have a religion, they need to be blessed with the 'only true religion' (a label which paradoxically each of the two religions claims for itself).

Chapter 13

The Young Acharya of Bageshwar

INDIA IS a special country. Where else do you find in every generation outstanding personalities who give spiritual and worldly guidance to the common people? The list is long. Very powerful gurus are on it and in all likelihood, the credit goes to them that over a thousand years, the invaders were not able to root out Sanatana Dharma, though efforts are still on.

Now again, a charismatic teacher has emerged. The young Acharya of Bageshwar Dham, Dhirendra Krishna Shastri inspires millions of common Hindus to pledge never to abandon their eternal dharma.

In August 2022, I was flying from Khajuraho to Delhi. Khajuraho is a small airport, and the passengers walk to the airplane. A woman, walking next to me, pointed to a young swami near us, 'We are so lucky', she said in a low voice. 'The Maharaj of Bageshwar Dham is flying with us. Thousands come for his *darshan*, and here we are so close to him.'

Till then, I had not heard of Dhirendra Krishna Shastri and Bageshwar Dham, but when I came home and showed the photo, which I had taken, to a neighbour, she exclaimed, 'You really have good karma to meet him personally. I love to watch his videos.'

A few months later, the young Bageshwar *Baba* was in the news for bringing back around 300 Christians to their original Hindu Dharma. While one hardly hears any objections in the media about the lakhs of Hindus who are regularly converted by Christian missionaries, *Gharwapsi* (home-coming) is usually portrayed as 'controversial', when it should be the other way round.

Soon after, an organisation against blind belief went after Dhirendra Shastri challenging his miraculous powers. The group even made a police complaint against him. However, it was dismissed as unfounded. The media, too, tried to discredit him by labelling him a 'self-styled god-man', even though he sees himself as a Hanuman bhakta, and says that his powers are only thanks to Hanuman ji.

When he announced a Hanuman *Katha* in Bihar in May 2023, the ruling political class in the state tried to prevent it and dismissed him as a nobody. Yet the reception that the twenty-six-year-old got in Bihar, was simply unbelievable. A crowd of ten lakh came to hear him. He had to ask those present at the large venue, NOT to come in the following days so as to give others a chance to hear him.

I watched his katha on TV. The crowds were unmanageable even in front of his hotel. It must have sent shivers down the spines of those politicians, who had staunchly opposed him.

What makes him special?

Probably this: Finally, here is a Hindu Baba who is giving a voice to Hindus whose faith is either intentionally or ignorantly demeaned the world over, including by several

Hindus, themselves. It seems, common Hindus were longing for someone who is solidly rooted in their eternal dharma, so much so, that he has accessed spiritual powers. They were longing for someone who does not care about political correctness but speaks up for Hinduism—a faith which no doubt has proven to be more beneficial for humanity than Abrahamic religions.

His supernatural powers to know the details and problems of the persons who come to him before they tell him anything, and the efficacy of his blessings to solve these problems, helped in making him immensely popular—even though the so-called 'educated' Hindu dismissed the possibility of the Baba being blessed with supernatural powers in their intellectual minds. They don't realise that theirs is a country full of genuine miracles and their disbelief in anything supernatural is the result of the British agenda to cut off Indians from their roots.

On the other hand, the Baba from Bageshwar Dham is forthright: 'India was, is, and will be a Hindu *Rashtra*,' he asserts. Apart from this, he advocates gharwapsi of those who had converted to Islam and Christianity—religions, which the foreign invaders brought with them to India.

'Don't just come and listen to the story of Ram and Hanuman. Come home to your ancient tradition,' he urged tribals in Gujarat, the state he visited after his Bihar programme. The Christian missionaries have made huge inroads there, mostly by giving goodies or frightening the tribals with stories of eternal hellfire.

His appeal makes a lot of sense, but so far, such an appeal has not been made in front of the cameras. This is strange, because all those rooted in Hindu Dharma and who know the negative sides of Abrahamic religions, are aware that Hindu

Dharma is far more preferable because of its inclusive nature and its profound philosophy.

Yet, even the famous swamis with huge, worldwide followings have not made this appeal so far. Sometimes, they even encourage Christians to 'become better Christians' and Muslims to 'become better Muslims'. They do not realise that a 'good' believer in the dogmas of those religions becomes a danger to Hindus, because that person's religion teaches him to despise them. According to the Bible and the Quran, Hindus are despicable heathens or *kafirs*, because they are idol-worshippers.

Why would Hindu swamis hesitate to ask converts to come back to their original faith? Is it due to the still colonised Indian mindset?

Or, is it due to fear that such an appeal could go against secularism and may even be illegal?

Unfortunately, after Independence, neither politics, nor the educational curriculum was friendly towards the Hindu tradition. Instead, they were distinctly more friendly towards the new religions. Convent schools were allowed to teach in Independent India. The Hindu administrators probably didn't even know that a 'good' Christian teacher despises Hinduism and conveys this in a subtle way to Hindu students.

There was no discussion about what Hinduism stands for. No discussion about Vedanta's profound philosophy, which claims that the multiplicity in this universe is a temporary appearance on the one eternal Brahman which is pure, blissful awareness.

Vedanta not only inspired Western philosophers, but also top scientists of quantum physics. Yet Indian students were taught that Hindu Dharma is inferior to Abrahamic religions.

Consequently, massive, fraudulent conversions were tolerated.

The great value of Hindu Dharma for humanity was played down, and even forgotten over time, as many Hindus became more and more ignorant about their tradition. They continued the worship of deities and started believing what Abrahamic religions claimed, that Hinduism is polytheistic idol-worship and nothing else.

However, in recent times, a change is happening, including among the Hindu youth. They discovered the serious drawbacks of Abrahamic religions, which instill a divisive, irrational mindset: 'Either you believe in our God and in His son/prophet, or you burn for all eternity in hellfire.'

In contrast, Hindu Dharma maintains: 'There are different flowers in God's garden and different ways to reach the Divine. He will not discard anyone into eternal hell. In fact, all are contained in Him, and all will be given chance after chance, in life after life.'

Yet strangely, of all the religions, Hinduism alone is singled out for attacks even in India. The Church plans to make India a Christian nation and the Muslim clergy plans to make India a Muslim nation.

Why are they so intent in pushing their religion on Hindus? Because they believe that it's the command of the Almighty.

This needs to be challenged.

Meanwhile, the Western world, and also India, have reached a stage, where Hindu Dharma urgently needs to be strengthened to stop widespread violence and massive moral degradation.

Otherwise, the goal of Islam, Christianity, and Communism—to eradicate Hinduism and its knowledge about our divine essence—may be achieved. This would be a disaster for humanity. So, the only hope for Hindu India to survive is that those who converted, should realise the drawbacks of their newly adopted religions, lose faith in them, and come back home (gharwapsi).

Therefore, the appeal of Dhirendra Krishna for gharwapsi is timely and comes like a breath of fresh air. There is hope now because at least the goal has been defined.

Yet one more issue needs to be tackled. The wisdom of the rishis needs to again reach the masses. Only when it is clear that Hindu Dharma is indeed superior, will those, who had converted, want to come back. Here the swami of Bageshwar Dham also does his bit, by explaining in simple terms how maya clouds our vision of who we really are.

Great wisdom is contained in the Hindu traditions—especially the liberating wisdom of Oneness of the individual's Atma (Self) with the infinite, eternal Brahman. Those who try to control humanity, may not want this knowledge to reach the common man because then it would liberate him from fear and he will not be easily controlled or enslaved.

These forces have great powers over the media. False allegations could be spread against the young Dhirendra Shastri. He would not be the first prominent Hindu to endure such injustice.

Let's hope, this won't happen and that with the blessings of Hanuman, Acharya Dhirendra Krishna Shastri will succeed in spreading the eternal Sanatana Dharma.

Chapter 14

Miracles are Possible
My Experience

IT SURPRISED me that some 'educated' Indian friends were critical of Dhirendra Krishna Shastri of Bageshwar Dham and especially of his miraculous powers. They suspected him of cheating. My Western friends were more open towards the possibility of miracles.

I got the feeling that the immense importance which Hindus generally give to education, has a downside:

During the time of the Gurukuls, when Gurus taught worldly and spiritual knowledge to their students, this focus on education was a great boon for Bharat and her people. Yet, when the British replaced the Gurukuls with their education system, Hindu parents didn't realise that their children would be taught a materialistic worldview where there would be no place for spirituality and the possibility of different dimensions of reality.

Therefore, it seems to be very difficult for educated Hindus to accept the possibility of inexplicable miracles, and even more difficult than for Westerners, as in the Indian tradition, teachers are not questioned.

Here is my personal experience of an amazing miracle by an 'ordinary' sadhu that cannot be explained.

In 2021, the festival of Maha Shivaratri was on 11 March. I was at the Kumbh Mela in Haridwar and an amazing incident happened on that day. I share it here, because I feel it can be inspiring and may help in judging sadhus more positively.

I was standing at the roadside with other people, watching the *Akhara* of the *Naga Sadhus* passing by to Har-ki-Pauri for their bath in the Ganga. There were some Babas on horses, some in carts, while the majority walked, most of them naked and smeared with ash, while some were wrapped in saffron cloth.

One of the naked Babas stopped in front of me and asked for Rs 100 which I gave him and he walked on.

A little while later, a saffron clad sadhu stopped before me and also asked for Rupees 100. I opened my purse and gave him a note of Rs 50 and one of Rs 20.

He said '*Tees kam hain*' (Rs 30 are less).

I told him that I don't have Rs 100, only a Rs 200 note. Could he give me back the change?

He said, 'I will give—*mai de dunga.*'

So, now he had three paper bills—Rs 20, 50, and 200.

He put them one above the other and folded them small. Then he asked me to open my hand and he put this small paper parcel into my hand and asked me to close it and keep it closed.

Yet, I opened my fist quickly and the folded paper notes opened again.

He folded the three bills again, placed them again into my palm and told me to keep my fist closed.

After some 4 or 5 seconds, the paper in my hand suddenly felt different, somehow smooth. I opened my hand and lo.... I couldn't believe it, there was a small Shivalingam in my palm. It had replaced those three notes.

A couple from Kutch, Gujarat, who had been standing next to me were also stunned. In fact, the wife spontaneously moved away several steps and told me later, that she was frightened of such sadhus. The sadhu said a few things, but I don't remember what. Then he joined the others and continued on his way.

I was glad that at first I had opened my hand quickly, as I could see that there were really the paper bills in it. Otherwise, I might have doubted, that maybe he had distracted me and put the Lingam into my hand, though I could feel the paper.

The next day, I attended the Aarti in the Ashram of Anandamayi Ma, at Kankhal and afterwards went into the Ashram shop. I did not look for it nor did I expect it, but right near the entrance, there were some plastic pouches with the same small Shivalingas.

I asked the price. Each was priced at Rs 160.

The sadhu had said that he would give me back the change and had kept his promise, plus minus Rs 10.

But I have no idea what happened to the money—if or how it reached him.... Nor do I have any idea how the Shivalingam got into my closed fist.

Nor do I know why the two sadhus had asked for Rs 100 when they were on their way to take a dip in the Ganga in this huge crowd. Surely, they would not have held onto that piece of paper?

There are so many things that we do not know....

Chapter 15

A Victory for Hindus after 500 Years of Struggle

ON 22 January 2024, there was a grand celebration in Bharat, and not only in Ayodhya. The happiness was palpable. Temples everywhere gave Prasadam (sacred food) and broadcast on large screens the Prana Pratishtha function that was taking place in Ayodhya.

Yet typically, the Western media was critical, and warned of 'Hindu supremacy' and was blatantly dishonest by hiding the fact that an ancient temple had been destroyed 500 years ago by Muslim invaders who had then built a mosque on top of it as a sign of their dominance.

On 22 January 2024, something huge was happening in Bharat after 500 long years. Common sense says that it should have happened much earlier. In 1947, when India was partitioned on religious lines, and Indians who had converted to Islam had got Pakistan, at that time, it would have been natural for Hindus to get back their temples which had been destroyed by invaders and mosques had been built over them, as symbols of dominance and supremacy.

But maybe, now the time is just right for Bharat, and the whole world, to install Sri Ram again in a grand *mandir* (temple) at his birthplace after a 500-year long struggle. The reason is: Sri Ram is the epitome of dharma, who fought and vanquished *adharmic* forces. In our times, too, *adharma* has become exceptionally strong. Divine help is urgently needed in fighting and vanquishing these adharmic forces.

Presently, humanity is not in good shape. It is without roots and direction, without meaning and values. It's called 'Being woke' and is even portrayed as positive. It spread among Westerners and already shows some impact among young Indians.

Truth as such has now been declared as non-existent, because 'everyone has his own truth'. There is no objective meaning to life either. It's now a 'personal matter'. To be selfish is considered the way to go.

Further, humans are being dumbed down with junk food, drugs, and low-grade entertainment and pornography, which benefits the producers of such content, but harms the consumers.

The belief in a Supreme Being and a soul has been ridiculed by 'renowned' philosophers and scientists. This includes the likes of popular writers like Yuval Noah Harari whose books sell millions of copies or scientists like Stephen Hawking.

Many more terrible things, which up to now were hidden, are coming to light thanks to social media and whistleblowers.

The worst of these things, is probably the massive scale of child trafficking—for sex abuse, organ and blood harvesting, and even for ritualistic 'sacrifices' (murder) to propitiate demonic forces by members of secret societies, who hold powerful positions in society.

It's all so unbelievable, but several whistleblowers had mysterious deaths soon after speaking up, and sadly, this gives them credibility.

The eternal strife between Devas (unselfish forces of goodness and light) and Asuras (selfish, dark, demonic forces) is underway since ancient times in this world of maya, and presently, the Asuras seem to have the upper hand. Lust, anger, and greed, the three gates to the hell of self-destruction according to Sri Krishna in the Bhagavad Gita (Chapter 16, verse 21) are rampant. Clearly, attempts are being made to cut off humans from their Atma, their divine Self, the worst thing that can possibly happen.

In the midst of this dark scenario, Bharat is still a beacon of light, even though here too, *Kali Yug* shows its effects. Yet, most Indians still have faith in dharma and in their Gods. They still know that they need to live life in a dharmic way and do what is right according to their conscience and scriptures. And, they still know about their divine core (Atma) and they are still devoted to the powerful, selfless Devas.

Bharat is the only place on earth, where daily, in thousands of temples, the Devas are worshipped for the well-being of ALL, and NOT the Asuras or satanic forces for personal wealth, fame, power, and sense-enjoyment. Every morning and evening, the temples reverberate with Aarti for the Lord of the world (*Om Jaya Jagadisha Hare…*) or for the deities of the particular temple, who are essentially all one with the ONE great Brahman.

The deities are not somewhere in heaven, but present in the temples due to the *Pran Pratishtha* having been performed, where the stone idol is infused with *prana*, the divine life-force.

On 22 January 2024, a special Pran Pratishtha was

finally performed after a 500 year-long wait: Sri Ram became a living presence in the newly-constructed grand Ram Mandir in Ayodhya.

Ayodhya—the name, itself, evokes great emotions in Hindus.

Ayodhya is the place where Lord Ram was born, and grew up with his brothers Lakshman, Bharat, and Shatrughna; where Sage Vashishta taught them the ancient wisdom, and Sage Vishwamitra took Ram and his brother Lakshman to fight the malevolent Asuras, who greatly troubled the Devas.

It is the place, where he brought Sita as his wife from Janakpur; from where he, along with Sita and Lakshman, left for his long exile on the very same day when his coronation was planned.

It is the place where his father died of grief because of the separation from his dearest son; where his brother Bharat ruled, putting the *padukas* (sandals) of Ram on the throne... and to which Ram returned with Sita, Lakshman, and Hanuman after he had defeated the demon king Ravana in Lanka, and established the benevolent Ram Rajya.

Every Hindu knows the details of Ram's life. The Ramayana is ingrained in them. It is played on village stages, chanted in ashrams and was an absolute hit on TV when it was first aired as a serial almost forty years ago. It is a sacred scripture that contains all that one needs to know about living a dignified life, and to behave in an ideal way in the midst of challenges.

Sri Ram is an outstanding example for humans—noble, just, brave, ever protecting the weak, and keeping his word.

And he is dearly loved by all Hindus.

Therefore, is there any question at all why Hindus fought for 500 years to get back this very special place and sacrificed so much? They fought against the Muslim invaders, who destroyed his temple, killed thousands of Hindus who defended it, and built a mosque on top of it.

In recent decades, they also had to fight against their own people—scheming politicians, communists, and former Hindus who had converted to Islam, who all denied that Ram was real and that there was even a mandir earlier at the same site.

Yet, finally, this is now past.

Bharat was celebrating. Many Hindus had taken vows in the run-up to the Pran Pratishtha, to purify themselves for the historic occasion. *Japa* of the Ram mantra was done and soul-stirring devotional bhajans were sung or listened to.

Prime Minister Narendra Modi, who was at the Pran Pratishtha ceremony had also followed certain rituals for 11 days prior to the ceremony. He said, 'I have to awaken Divine Consciousness in myself, too'. As Prime Minister, he has tremendous responsibilities. Surely, he needs and will ask for guidance from *Prabhu* Sri Ram.

Typically, the Western media criticised PM Modi for being so unapologetically Hindu. They wondered, what is it about Hindu Dharma which makes people stick to it, in spite of all the negative propaganda against it by Abrahamic religions, by communists, and the media. Why are the attacks on Hinduism from all sides not working as planned? Why do even now more and more Hindus treasure their heritage? Why do even many foreigners consider Hindu Dharma the best option for humanity and the world?

The answer is easy: Hindu Dharma is based on truth and righteous living. It tells us who we really are in our essence (eternal Atma). And in this temporary world of maya, it is on the side of Devas, who want to liberate us from maya by realising our divine Consciousness, and not on the side of those who want to drive us deeper into ignorance and bondage.

Yet there is still a big challenge for Bharat: How to make those Indians who have been completely indoctrinated to look down on the faith of their Hindu ancestors—either by their newly adopted religions or by the education system—also see this truth?

Hopefully, Sri Ram will give *sadbuddhi* (right insight) to all. And, may all feel His Divine Presence in their hearts....

Jai Sri Ram!

Chapter 16

Kanwar Mela in Haridwar

I HAD sent a picture of the massive crowd at the Kanwar Mela in Haridwar to a Christian friend in Germany. She was simply amazed about the fact that so many young men had come to the Mela. 'Of such huge gatherings, we can only dream', she replied. 'Yesterday we were five people attending the mass in church. Of those five, one was the priest and another his assistant…'

All over India, an interesting phenomenon can be observed. On the one hand, materialism is on the rise, and on the other, the popularity of rituals and religious festivals is also very much on the rise. Even festivals like the Kanwar Mela, which involve great hardships and attract huge crowds, most of them, young men. It indicates that in spite of the modern lifestyle of the Indians and the Western influence on them, their bond to the ancient spiritual dimension is strong. A majority of Indians still feel connected with the invisible power that is behind the visible forms and to the Gods who represent this power.

In Dehradun, where I live, I got the impression that the

Kanwar Mela is mainly about traffic jams and rowdies, who want to have a good time. Several of my English-educated, Western-oriented acquaintances talked condescendingly about the *Kanwarias*. They considered them a big nuisance who take-over the highways and create huge traffic jams.

Maybe, among the many million Kanwarias who come to take Ganga water from Haridwar over the first fortnight of the month of *Shravan* (July/August), there are some troublemakers too. Yet from my experience, the Kanwarias are amazingly good-natured, and they are the ones who have a hard time.

Of course, the people of Haridwar also have to put up with great inconveniences, especially towards the end of the *mela*, when most of those Kanwarias, who walk the whole distance on foot back to their homes, have left the city and others on motorcycles and trucks with loud music blaring, move in. Around 50,000 vehicles enter the city on each of the last three days.

In recent years, the number of Kanwarias has exploded. In 2023, more than 40 million had come into a town of 250,000 inhabitants. The huge crowds everywhere take a toll on the city's infrastructure, but, the genuine friendliness and cheerfulness of the Kanwarias stand out all the more. The citizens of Haridwar calmly bear the teeming crowds. They know the reason why they come to their holy city and respect the Kanwarias. And many benefit financially as well.

I went to Haridwar during the early days of the mela. Coming in by train, which overlooked some of the city roads, I was presented with a spectacular view. As my sister called from Germany just then, I gave her a running commentary of the milling crowds, mainly young men dressed in saffron-hued T-shirts and shorts. I am sure, she could not have pictured it.

We simply don't have an equivalent of this festival in the West.

Maybe that is the reason why I appreciate and enjoy the atmosphere in India and my Western-oriented Indian friends do not. They seem to be irritated and embarrassed by such display of religious fervour. Maybe they feel that it shows India in a poor light. They don't realise that this living spirituality is what makes India special in the international community.

The Western attitude of ignoring and even denying the invisible power behind the visible has made our lives empty and barren. When we are not connected to the spiritual dimension, natural joy, cheerfulness, and solid grounding in human values are lacking. It is no surprise that mental depression is so rampant in Western societies.

In the West, we try hard 'to have a good time' during the weekends and holidays. There are several options, like going out for meals, visiting a picturesque town, walking around street festivals, going to a lake for a swim, or into the mountains for trekking, and of course, the one thing many people live for—going for the yearly holiday to some far-away exotic country. Indeed, we may have a good time, provided nothing gets on our nerves. But at the same time, a sense of futility creeps in. Back from a holiday, everyone is likely to say how wonderful it was. But for many, it turns wonderful only in retrospect, while boasting before friends.

In India, celebration and enjoyment are ingrained in the culture and mostly connected with the Divine. Almost all festivals have a religious nature. A Beer festival like the Munich Oktoberfest is simply out of place in Bharat. Or egg-throwing competitions, and competitions about who can eat or drink the most in the shortest time, that happen regularly in the West.

In India, the Divine power and sacredness are taken for real and the tradition of doing *tapas* (austerities) is very much alive. The Kanwar Mela is all in one: enjoyment, bonding with family and friends, adventure, trekking, devotion, and participating in severe tapas (i.e., sacrificing one's own personal comfort as an offering to the Divine).

There is a sense of purpose. In the back of one's mind, there is the link with Lord Shiva. *Bam Bam Bhole* and *Jai Shiv Shankar* reverberate in the atmosphere. There is still the acknowledgment, if not a sense of wonder and love, regarding the invisible power behind the visible forms.

This attitude makes Indians cultured, even if they come from very poor backgrounds. They have certain guidelines that they stick to, and being good-natured and accommodating towards others are two of these guidelines. This is not so in the West. Egoism is the main guiding force there. I remember a discussion in a psychology class on whether it is good to be selfless. No, it is not good, because to express and push through one's own needs is most important to stay psychologically healthy, was the consensus.

In Haridwar, I watched the unending stream of Kanwarias walking back home, carrying fancily decorated bamboo structures, called *kanwars*, that contained vessels filled with *Gangajal* (Ganga water). They continued walking with their heavy load even in pouring rain. Several wore crepe bandages around their calf muscles and ankles. One young man, barefoot, was limping. Even one blister would make every step painful. Two handicapped men pedalled along in their decorated wheelchairs. Some middle-aged men did not carry the kanwars but had two containers with Gangajal hanging around their necks. Although tired, they all smiled easily and waved, while I took pictures.

Strangely, twenty-five years ago, there was no Kanwar Mela in Haridwar. Traditionally, Kanwarias have been associated with Baidyanath Dham in today's Jharkhand. How did it happen that the Kanwar Mela became such a huge event in Haridwar after the Kumbh Mela, the biggest religious gathering, worldwide?

'You know, in Hinduism, we don't have fixed rules about how to worship. Everyone is free to do as they please,' an old Haridwar resident answered my question. 'During the Holy month of Shravan, there were always people coming to Haridwar to take a dip in the Ganga and then they would offer Gangajal in the local Shiva temples here or go to Neelkanth Mahadev temple near Rishikesh.

'At one point, someone must have gotten the idea to carry the Ganga water all the way back to his hometown. Then next year, more people did it and so on. And now there are many million people who carry Gangajal home to their respective Shiva temples to offer it there on *Shivaratri*, the night before the new moon in the Shravan month. A new form of worship had taken birth,' he chuckled.

In Hinduism, this flexibility on worship allows changes that are in tune with the times. Nowadays, many pilgrims make use of trucks and vans, but in an original way. The trucks are only a support system.

It works like this:

Relatives or villagers get together and rent a truck for the pilgrimage. Cooking utensils, stoves, provisions, sleeping mats, and so forth are carried in the back of the truck, and a wooden platform above the luggage is packed with pilgrims. Once the holy water is taken from the Ganga, it is not placed in the truck, but instead, reverentially carried on foot in a relay by the young men in the group. At least one man at a time runs behind the truck with a kanwar over his shoulder, and when he is tired, another man takes over. This gives the older people and those, who are doubtful whether they can walk long distances, a chance to be part of the mela.

Undoubtedly, most of the Kanwarias are not used to walking long distances, yet this does not prevent most of them from making the resolve to go on foot. One group, that I met, had come from Meerut. They had planned to cover the 175 km-distance in three days. There were several women, stoically walking along. Apart from the kanwar, many seemed to carry nothing else. Some carried a small backpack. One group had a cart that was packed with children and was pulled by a cycle, while the adults walked alongside.

From where I watched the stream of pilgrims, they had not yet walked ten kilometres. How will they feel after 100 km? It is certainly an arduous journey. Along the route, several Hindu organisations and even individuals offer food and shelter to the Kanwarias.

'These facilities were not there in the olden days,' a man from Bihar told me. In 1965, as a twenty-year-old, he had walked the 120 kilometres from Sultangunj to Baidyanath Dham. 'The path through the hilly terrain was very rough, and often littered with pebbles as sharp as needles and we all walked barefoot. I had blisters as big as cricket balls,' he remembered.

'Did you wish for something from Shiva?' I asked.

'No, I had gone in thanksgiving. I had promised to do the pilgrimage if a certain thing would happen. It happened and I fulfilled my vow,' he explained.

Many of the Kanwarias come to thank Shiva for fulfilling some desire, while others come to ask for some favours. For many, it is a special sort of outing, physically demanding, yet ultimately far more fulfilling, thanks to the heartfelt connection with their beloved Shiva, than simply 'having a good time'.

Chapter 17

The Value of Bhajans (in Euros)

AT RELIGIOUS festivals in India, there are many opportunities to attend a *Bhajan* session. Yet, did you ever wonder about the value of bhajans? Some of the great spiritual masters value it highly. Especially in Kali Yuga, it is said that bhajans are an easy way to connect with the Divine. Somehow, I took it for granted, that there is no fee for attending a bhajan session. After all, the lead singer benefits as much, if not more, as those who follow him or her. Everyone simply expresses their devotion in a joyful manner.

Some years ago, when I was visiting Germany, a magazine for which I wrote, invited me to a *Concert of Indian Music* in Munich. The artiste was an American. I had no idea what to expect, but I happily accepted the invitation.

On the evening of the concert, around 200 people had gathered at the auditorium in Munich—some of them obviously former hippies who had been to India, but the majority were 'normal' Germans, who were not happy when they were asked to remove their shoes. Before entering the hall, we filed past a table where the tickets were being sold and a sheet of paper was handed out. The price of the ticket was 35 Euros, which equaled to roughly Rs 3,000. I was glad I had an invitation.

Then the artiste came, accompanied by a *tabla* player. He seemed likeable and started by telling us about his time in India in the 1970s, when he had met his Guru Neemkaroli Baba in Kainchi near Nainital, while living with an Indian family. Every evening, this family sang *bhajans* and he enjoyed it. Occasionally, the grandfather would stop singing and go straight into *Samadhi*, the American said, while lifting his head to the ceiling and stretching out his arms, probably indicating to us the state of the Samadhi. 'That is the power of bhajans, if it is sung with full devotion and just for the joy of it,' he added.

After his short talk, the concert started. It turned out to be a bhajan session, with the American leading the way, and we full throatily joining in, thanks to the sheet of paper, where *Om Namah Shivaya, Hare Rama, Hare Krishna, Jai Durga* and so on was typed for the benefit of those who were not familiar with the Indian tradition. The American was a good singer with a pleasant voice. Soon the atmosphere was charged, with most of us singing loudly and clapping our hands to the rhythm.

When it was over, there were happy faces all around. Nobody seemed to mind that actually they had performed for almost half of the 'concert' time, faithfully following whatever the artiste was singing. Nobody seemed to mind that they had paid quite a lot, and that the lead singer would have got quite a lot.

A friend, who had accompanied me and who had never been to a bhajan session before, also enjoyed it and straightaway headed for the counter where CDs of the bhajan singer were being sold. It was only my small mind which started calculating and concluded that a sum of about Rs 6 lakh must have been collected from that one and a half hour of bhajan-singing.

It suddenly struck me that hardly anyone in the West has the chance to sing loudly and clap hands to joyful songs that are directed to the Divine. In fact, most Germans probably do not even know the text of a single song which they could sing, if given a chance. Singing and clapping are the most basic expressions of joy! Even if there is no joy felt at the outset of a bhajan, doesn't it come at least to some extent in the wake of it? Worries have no space to intrude into your mind at this time; one is present in the now and enjoys it.

I guess those Germans felt this joy and willingly paid 35 Euros to be able to sing along with the bhajan singer.

Now, since the value of bhajans is known even in monetary terms, aren't we lucky in Bharat? Most of us not only have a big repertoire of songs but also many opportunities to go for free bhajan sessions where we can sing wholeheartedly and express our devotion in the company of others.

Maybe this is one of the reasons why the atmosphere generally feels light in India and a smile comes easily to Indians, despite the many difficult circumstances that they have to face.

Chapter 18

Is Buddhism Intellectual, and Hinduism Superstitious?

SOME TEN years ago, I met an American from Seattle, who had studied Sanskrit at the university there. He had come to India to meet his Guru and had taken an Indian name. He told me that Westerners, including professors at his university, who had accepted Buddhism, had no hesitation in openly identifying as Buddhists, yet those, who felt close to Hinduism, would not readily identify themselves as Hindus. He summed it up: to be a Buddhist makes you look intellectual in the eyes of others, but to be a Hindu makes you look somewhat suspect.

A few months after I had met this American, Julia Roberts openly declared that she is a practising Hindu, and I wondered whether those Americans now have more courage to stand by their convictions.

In India, the English educated elite seem to have taken a cue from the West, as they unfortunately often do. They also seem to feel that Buddhism is intellectual and Hinduism is suspect.

In 2008, Thich Nhat Hanh, a Buddhist monk from Vietnam, who lived in France and passed away in 2022, came to India to conduct workshops. He also came to Dehradun. I signed up and was amazed that many of the elite in town were present—people who would never listen to a Hindu swami.

The most reputed school in town, and maybe in the whole of India, the Doon School, had hosted the event. A big hotel catered the food. The hall was packed on the first evening. The Kendriya Vidyalayas, schools run by the Central Government, had dispatched two teachers each from their local schools to attend the workshop. Thich Nhat Hanh had come with a group of monks and nuns, dressed in dark, long robes who stood behind him and chanted before his lecture. It was impressive.

What the Buddhist monk said was good advice, but common knowledge and more attuned to Western societies, like 'If you have misunderstandings with your father, clear them before he dies.'

The attendance thinned out considerably over the three days of the workshop, in spite of the good food. Yet the teachers of the Kendriya Vidyalayas were stuck. I talked to them, and they felt that any Hindu swami could do the same, if not a better job. They had a point, as Thich Nhat Hanh made a few blunders, like when he mentioned, 'A French philosopher said that there is no death'. This French philosopher probably got his knowledge from the Bhagavad Gita.

Recently, a question was asked on *Quora*, why are not more Indians aware of Buddhism, even though Buddha was born in India.

I replied that Hinduism has many sages and Buddha was one of them. Many of those sages could have started an '–ism' in their names. Luckily, they did not. It is doubtful whether Buddha had approved of Buddh-ism. It was Emperor Ashoka a few hundred years after Buddha, who was intent on making people follow the Buddha.

Adi Shankara did his bit on the intellectual and spiritual level to restore the Hindu tradition by challenging the Buddhist scholars for debates and coming out of them convincingly.

A physical deadly blow was given by the Muslim invaders, especially under Muhammad Khilji around 1200 AD, who ransacked the Nalanda University which housed apart from Hindus, thousands of Buddhist monks from India and all over Asia. Thousands of monks were killed and the huge library was burned. It is said that it burned for three months. Imagine the wealth of knowledge that went up in flames, at a time, when the West had just started establishing universities.

Hinduism is a new term, introduced by the British, and does not do justice to the great variety of views, of philosophies, of Gods, of rituals and to the huge body of knowledge that is contained in the Vedas and the auxiliary works, which include 'worldly' subjects like medicine, economy, astronomy, mathematics, architecture, arts, and so on. In fact, Hindus don't see a dichotomy between the worldly and sacred. All is a manifestation of the one great, invisible Brahman or Ishwara.

Hindus don't feel the need to pledge that they will follow only one particular human being. They are free to choose what suits them best to connect with the Divine, which the Vedas claim is one's innermost essence. There is no need to identify with only one strand of the many possible helpful strands, which have emerged over many millennia.

An example from my experience: In my early years in India, most of the foreigners I met, identified themselves as Buddhists. Most of them also felt that Buddhism was superior to Hinduism. They were attending the teachings by their root

Lama. I met several of those Lamas.

Once, a French girl wanted me to join her and take initiation from a visiting high Tibetan Lama, who was the Guru of Sakya Trizin, the head of the Sakya-pa sect, who had his monastery in Dehradun, opposite to where I stayed at that time. It was clear that if one wanted to take initiation, one had to become a Buddhist by 'taking refuge in Buddha, Dharma, and Sangha'. So, I told her that I didn't want to limit myself and would rather keep my freedom. She felt I was missing a great chance and talked to the Lama. 'You can take part without taking refuge', she beamed. So, I did.

A few days later, I went with her to see Sakya Trizin. His first words were: 'Oh Maria, you are now a Buddhist.' My spontaneous reaction: 'No, I am not....'

In 1985, I had a chance, together with two German friends, to spend over an hour with the Dalai Lama in his bungalow in Dharamsala. I mentioned to him that I had met several Hindu sages and was greatly impressed by Indian philosophy.

The Dalai Lama then asked me, 'Do you think that the concept of Atma in Hinduism makes any difference to Buddhism?' I was sure that it does not and quoted from the Upanishads, *'Ayam Atma Brahman'* (This Atma is Brahman). However, I am not sure whether the Dalai Lama also saw it like this.

A few weeks later, I again saw Sakya Trizin, and asked him, 'What is the difference between Buddhism and Hinduism?' He immediately replied: 'The concept of Atma.'

Buddhist monks have to study many Buddhist texts, and I guess, to mark a basically non-existent border to Hinduism, they learn that Atma signifies a kind of separate entity. Some philosophers may see it like this, but Advaita Vedanta does not.

Hindus respect Buddha. He is even seen as an avatar. He is one of their own. Hindus do not feel the need for a demarcation to other views. They are the least dogmatic of all and have the most profound philosophy as a solid basis for the manifold ways of connecting with all-pervading Divinity for which (though formless and nameless) they have varied names, the foremost being Brahman. Buddhist philosophy is based on Hindu philosophy. The only difference is in the terminology. After all, 'Truth is One'.

Chapter 19

Is there Rivalry Between Buddhism and Hinduism?

PRINCE SIDDHARTHA, who was later called 'Buddha', was a Hindu. He didn't promote Buddhism. Emperor Ashoka, who was born a few centuries later, was the one who promoted Buddhism. He wanted his subjects to follow what Buddha had taught and what was compiled in some councils, long after Buddha's death.

The story goes that Ashoka felt so much repentance after a cruel war that he converted to Buddhism. Yet another version says that as he had killed his brother to get to the throne, he was censored by a Brahmin council. Consequently, he declared himself a Buddhist, even before that brutal war.

Whatever may be the reason for his conversion, the fact is that it needs force to push a new faith onto people, and Ashoka used force, especially against Jains and Brahmins. It also needs the claim that the new faith is better than the old one, otherwise, why would people change their faith?

A few centuries later, Christianity and Islam repeated this recipe of using force and unsubstantiated claims with grave consequences for humanity. Luckily Buddhism didn't have such a negative outcome because Buddha's teachings were basically Hindu teachings, which does not divide humanity into those who are saved and those who are damned, depending on what one believes. Moreover, most Indian Buddhists reverted to Hinduism after some centuries, and many were killed in the brutal Muslim invasions. Yet Buddhism survived in other Asian countries.

Today, we can observe that Buddhists insist that theirs is a different religion, whereas Hindus don't see much difference.

To justify their claim that Buddhism is a separate religion, Buddhists often try to find 'differences' in regard to Hinduism. My Buddhist foreign friends tried to explain the big difference to me: in Buddhism, there is no self, whereas Hinduism postulates a self (Atma). Their conclusion was: That is why Buddhism is closer to the truth.

However, these differences are not real.

Atma in Hinduism is usually translated as 'Self'. Yet, the Upanishads clearly state that Atma is Brahma(n). This means that there is no separate self. All is the one, pure Consciousness, called Brahman or *Paramatma*.

What Buddhists call 'Clear Mind' or Nirvana, the Vedas call Brahman, Paramatma, or simply *Tat* (That). The terminology is different, but the truth is the same. So, it means that there is a slight rivalry, and in some cases, even a massive rivalry.

For example, I once read very negative, even abusive, comments on Hinduism by a Sri Lankan Buddhist monk. He was then asked by one of his disciples, 'But isn't Hinduism the mother of Buddhism?' The monk's reply: 'Even a bad mother can have a good son'. I remember it, because it shocked me.

Today also, the attempt to look superior exists on social

media, for example on Twitter (now X). There are some handles which not only stress the supremacy of Buddhism but also demonise Hinduism. For example, they claim that Hindus had brutally exterminated the Buddhists in India, when in fact it was done by Muslim invaders. Hindus even protected the temple in Bodh Gaya, where Buddha had gained enlightenment, when Buddhists abandoned it, as the monks were killed by Muslims and nobody was there to take care of it. Meanwhile, it is again looked after by Buddhists.

So, there is rivalry, but only from the Buddhists' side, because they need to justify why they are not one of the many branches of Hinduism, but are instead, a separate religion altogether.

If Buddhists allowed it, Hinduism would have no problem in integrating Buddhism as one more branch of the vast Sanatana Dharma.

Chapter 20

What is Religion Good For?

IN MANY parts of Europe, religion has become an important topic only in the last few decades. In the 1970s, religion or rather Christianity, which meant religion then, seemed outdated. It was considered something appropriate for children and old women. Ever since Christians were allowed to leave the Church not so long ago (less than 200 years ago in northern Germany), many did so.

Just an example: When I was a child in the 1950s, in our small town, mass was held daily at 6.30 am, at 7 am, and three times a week at 8 am. Since long now, there is not even one daily mass. Only the three services at 8 am have survived and those too have been shifted to 9 am.

In the 1950s, three hours of fasting were mandatory before taking Holy Communion. Now it has been scaled down to half an hour.

Earlier, missing Sunday Mass was a grave sin that would be punished with hell fire. Now, one can attend mass on Saturday instead of Sunday.

Christianity seemed on its way out, yet suddenly, 'religion' is not only back but is very prominent in the public discourse. The main reason is the increasing visibility of Islam in Europe.

In the 1960s, when the first Muslim Turks came to Germany (called 'Guest-workers'), especially young Germans (including me) were happy that our boringly uniform society had turned 'multicultural', with more interesting looking people on the streets. This enthusiasm has dimmed considerably. Former chancellor Angela Merkel admitted that the multicultural experiment has failed completely, and I suspect, she knew it right from the start... yet she nevertheless, allowed from 2015 onwards, the big influx (some call it invasion) of mainly young, male Muslim refugees.

It is for the first time, after Christianity had crushed the pagan faith in Europe over a thousand years ago, that the locals are confronted with a substantial population of followers of a different religion, which, as aggressively as Christianity or even more, proclaims that it alone is the true religion, and whoever does not join it, will be damned to hell forever and would even deserve to die. Many of those followers take their religion very seriously.

This jolted the Germans who generally did not identify as Christians any longer. Now, many felt the need to counter Islam with Christianity. In 2011, Angela Merkel even invited the Pope to address the Parliament. Some years ago, while strolling through Munich city on a Sunday morning, I saw many, including fashionable youngsters, streaming into a big old church.

Even in the small town where my mother lived, I saw young parents take their children to church for the Sunday children's service. In the 1970s, this would have been an unusual sight, when those same parents would have opted for an outdoor picnic instead.

On social media, too, especially in USA, big influencers now identify more than ever as Christians or at least they acknowledge a higher power. The President of El Salvador, Nayib Bukele, said in an interview to Tucker Carlson in June 2024 that when he was faced with an impossible situation regarding drug gangs, which practised satanic rituals including child sacrifice, he and his cabinet prayed right there in the meeting for God's wisdom and help. Tucker was surprised, 'Did all agree?' 'Yes, all are believers in God,' Bukele replied.

What draws people to religion? What is it good for?

In all likelihood, the most important point is an intuition in humans that there is a higher, unfathomable power which is the cause for this universe and the cause for our existence.

There must be some intelligent cause because it is simply not possible that this creation happened by chance.

Further, there is an intuition that somehow, this intelligence knows us and even guides us in our life by this small voice called our conscience. It prods us to choose good over evil, light over darkness. There is an inner communion possible, be it through prayer or a feeling of awe.

This intuition makes sense, is natural, and is even logical. It does not require the label of 'religion' and for very long, it never had this label. The logical consequence of this intuition was to search for that intelligent power within oneself and outside. It prompted people to become mystics who pondered over what is really true.

We know that this went on for ages in Bharat, as many invaluable, ancient texts are preserved, which declare that this unfathomable power is pure, thought-free

Consciousness—Brahman.

However, in the last 4,000 years of our long human history, the invisible topmost Reality or, in other words, the underlying substratum of everything, called Brahman in the Vedas, was distorted into a personal, separate 'one' God.

In Zoroastrianism, the highest level of A-dvaita (not-two), the impersonal Oneness of Brahman, is no longer present. It considers Ahura Mazda as the Supreme God who stands for goodness.

The worshippers of Ahura Mazda were opposed to *Daeva* worshippers. One could assume, that Daeva stands for Deva and the 'Devas versus Asuras' dichotomy of Sanatana Dharma had been inverted as Ahura versus Daeva in Zoroastrianism. However, this is not the case. Prof Subhash Kak writes in his book *The Idea of India*[5] that there was actually a tripartition in ancient Bharat: *Devas, Asuras, Rakshasas,* that corresponded to Sattva, Rajas, Tamas. Interestingly, *Rakshasas,* who have demonic qualities, are called *Daevas* or *Daivas* (not to confuse with Devas) in Kashmir. So there is no inversion of the Deva versus Asura dichotomy, but rather a focus on the dichotomy of Asura (Ahura) versus Rakshasa (Daeva).

The Daevas mentioned in Zoroastrian texts are clearly negative forces, comparable to Rakshasas, and those who worshiped them with abhorrent rituals, were fought. Prof Kak

---

5 *The Idea of India* by Subhash Kak, Garuda Prakashan, 2023

mentions that King Xerxes of Persia who ruled from 485 to 465 BCE proclaimed that he had destroyed a sanctuary where a Daiva was worshipped and had ordered: 'The Daiva shall not be worshipped!'.

But Daiva worshippers survived in an area south of the Caspian Sea, which stretched up to the Mediterranean Sea. Are they possibly the Canaanites whom the God of the Old Testament wanted to be utterly destroyed?

In Judaism, Yahweh, had become definitely personal and even jealous and revengeful. Here also, the highest Advaita level is missing.

Jews believe that they are Yahweh's chosen people whom He had guided to the promised land Canaan. Yahweh wanted the seven tribes, who lived in Canaan, when the Israelites arrived, completely destroyed, including their children and cattle, because of their detestable practices for their Gods. From the Israelites, Yahweh demanded obedience to His Ten Commandments which He gave to Moses on Mount Sinai. The first of them mandates, 'You shall not have other Gods before me'.

So, does it mean that Yahweh is a powerful tribal God who is committed to the welfare of the Israelites? One who wanted to prevent the Israelites to follow the 'Gods' of the Canaanites, who were demonic and even demanded children to be sacrificed?

Judaism's offspring, Christianity, proclaimed in the New Testament, a kinder God than the vengeful God of the Old Testament—a God who is for everyone and not specifically for Jews. Jesus harshly criticised the scribes and pharisees of his own Jewish community for leaving the right path which Moses had asked them to follow. He even called the Father of the Jews the devil (John 8:44) and finally paid for it with his life.

Intriguingly, Jesus preached certain aspects of Vedic wisdom, like 'The kingdom of heaven is within you', 'I and my Father are one' or 'As you sow, so shall you reap'. He also strongly advocated bhakti. Once, when asked what is the greatest commandment, he replied: 'You must love the Lord, your God with all your heart and all your soul and all your mind. This is the first and greatest commandment. And the second is: Love your neighbour as yourself' (Matthew 22: 37-39).

This teaching is very much in agreement with Sanatana Dharma and gives credence to the claim that Jesus was in India during the 'missing years' from the age of 12 to 30.

However, the influence of Saint Paul and the institution of the Church closed this open-mindedness and affinity to Hindu Dharma. The Church concluded that Jesus meant ONLY himself, when he said 'I and my Father are one' and therefore declared that the way to the Father and to salvation leads ONLY via Jesus Christ'. Accepting Jesus as the saviour of mankind was declared necessary to be eligible for heaven.

As soon as Christianity became the state religion of the Roman Empire, its followers forced their belief on the pagans of the vast areas in Middle East, North Africa, and Europe. The Christian God was now also 'jealous' of other Gods and the Church also, like Judaism, declared its first commandment as: 'You shall have no other Gods before me'. The question could be asked, whether already in its early stages, Christianity was subverted and made into an instrument of power? Did an equivalent of today's deep state exist back then?

A few hundred years later, another offspring of Judaism, Islam, claimed that God, now called 'Allah', had spoken through Prophet Mohammed for the very last time. That meant there were to be no more messages from the highest power in the future! Allah is very similar to the vengeful, jealous God of the Old Testament, but Allah doesn't look after Jews. He looks after only Muslims.

Muslims believe that Allah wants only Muslims on earth. Therefore, Muslims actively proselytise, apart from killing nonbelievers. The belief in Allah and his Prophet was declared a necessary condition to enter paradise.

It did not take long before the followers of those different Abrahamic branches were at each other's throats. Soon, Islam got the upper hand in many areas 'with fire and sword', as we can—sadly—vividly imagine. And of course, it did not bypass the wealthiest land on earth at that time—Bharat.

All those religions, which postulate a personal, separate God, don't have a solid philosophical basis. They consider something that can be thought of, and which is therefore an object to our Consciousness (or rather to us, because our essence is Consciousness) as the ultimate Creator of the universe. They stay on the level of Maya with its duality of good and evil, and cannot perceive That, which is beyond Maya, beyond name and form—Brahman or Sat-Chit-Ananda.

Christianity and Islam expanded their reach through violence, and kept their flock in check by brainwashing children and by threatening adults with severe punishments if they dared to disagree with the doctrine.

However, when Christianity lost its power to punish heretics during the era of enlightenment, it lost many followers in the West. It tries to compensate for this loss especially in India by luring followers with material benefits.

Judaism is the only Abrahamic religion that does not try to increase its numbers. The reason is that Jews claim that they have a Covenant with God and are chosen to rule the world. Most Jews, even if not religious, identify with their community. And, as a community, they are doing extremely well in the world: They have huge influence in big finance, big corporations, media, academia, entertainment, and in global politics. They also were the driving force in the communist revolution in Russia in 1917. So does it follow that they are, indeed, God's chosen people? Or, are there other reasons for their amazing worldly success?

An Orthodox Rabbi demanded from Netanyahu (a video clip is on the net) to speed up the process to fulfil the conditions for the arrival of their Messiah. One condition for his arrival is to build the third temple on the temple mount in Jerusalem, for which preparations are already underway. There is allegedly another, worrisome condition: a big war, called the *War of Gog and Magog*, that needs to happen before the Messiah comes. Are the wars in Ukraine and Gaza meant to expand into this big war? Or, is the stand-off between India and Pakistan meant to flare up, and even turn nuclear?

Nobody knows how many Muslims would leave Islam, if there were no blasphemy laws with severe punishments in place. I have heard expats from Iran say that it might even be a majority. Yet whenever required for the Deep State, Islam seems a convenient tool to create violence and turmoil in societies, including in Bharat. Not only Taliban, but even ISIS and Al Qaeda have been fostered by the Deep State's USAID, as investigations by the new US Department of Government Efficiency (*DOGE*) revealed.

The Hindu tradition is very different from those later religions. It does not have a founder. It does not favour only one group, but is truly universal. It has no blasphemy laws and does not need any. Proof is that even in the face of grave danger to their life under Muslim rule and of being exposed to ridicule under British rule, a majority of the Hindus held on to their tradition.

Why?

Because it makes sense.

First, it is not based on a story about a founder and what he said, but it is based on universal dharma—of doing the right thing at the right time in the given circumstances.

And second, because its philosophy with its two levels of Absolute Truth (Brahman, Oneness) and relative truth (maya, plurality) is solid.

Hindus pray for the welfare of all the worlds. Their 'great God' is not jealous. How could the Supreme Being be jealous? If it is jealous, it cannot be the topmost power. And indeed, there are some Christian and Jewish scholars who consider the 'God' of the monotheistic religions as lower 'Gods', more like angels or like the Devas of Hindu Dharma whom those religions so badly malign.

Unfortunately, in Independent India, an insidious teaching that 'All religions are the same' did a lot of harm and enticed many to convert for some benefits. If instead, a genuine debate between Hindus and followers of the Abrahamic religions had happened, those with an open mind would have realised that whatever new tenets the Abrahamic religions brought in (blind belief in what one person said; condemnation of those who don't believe it) was no improvement but a deterioration of the ancient Sanatana Dharma. And the most detrimental aspect: the Abrahamic religions made their followers forget that God is within themselves.

Chapter 21

Please Hindus, Don't Say 'All Religions are the Same'

FINALLY, HINDUS realised that they have been misled to believe that all religions are equal or even worse, and that their own Hindu tradition is inferior. Unfortunately, till a few decades ago, this belief was widespread.

Hindus used to say, 'All religions are equal'. They did not want to see that the two biggies, Christianity and Islam, did not agree. Each of those religions claimed, 'We alone are the only true religion. Our God is the only true God.' They pitied Hindus who believed that by stating that all religions are equal, Hinduism would be elevated to their level. Of course, these two religions will never allow this.

Then Hindus said, 'We respect all religions. We teach it to our children. Our children hear a lot about Christianity and Islam and how good these religions are. We don't want to offend anyone, so we teach very little and only about superficial things, like our festivals and customs. We do not teach the deep philosophy and the scientific insights which would portray Hinduism in a good light and might irritate other religions.'

Again, Hindus did not want to see that Christianity and Islam do not respect Hinduism. The clergy of those religions don't say it to their face, but to their own flock they say: 'Hindus go to hell if they don't convert to our true religion. It is their own fault. We have told them about Jesus and his Father or about the Prophet and Allah, respectively. Still, they are so arrogant and hold on to their false gods. But God/Allah is great. He will punish them with eternal hellfire.'

In a variation of 'We respect all religions' Hindus also say, 'All religions teach human beings to be virtuous and lead him to God'. Hindus attend Inter-Faith Dialogues and point to commonalities. Of course, there are common things. Hindus try to build on them. 'Yes, all religions have good points. Yes, all religions have good people.' They keep repeating that all religions teach goodness, as if to convince themselves.

However, deep down, Hindus know that this is not honest and lacks intellectual integrity. They know that Christianity and Islam have gone off-track by preaching exclusiveness and hatred for Hindus to their flock. Those religions have encouraged persecution of others and brainwashed otherwise kind human beings into fighting for an imaginary God who supposedly hates all those 'others'. They have left a trail of bloodshed in history.

But Hindus chose to ignore it. 'Why provoke unnecessarily?' they reason, still betraying a psyche that has been wounded by thousand years of oppression.

Is it not time that Hindus call a spade a spade?

Swami Vivekananda has said that every Hindu who leaves his faith is not one Hindu less but one enemy more. He said this while India was ruled by the British, and Christians and Muslims were encouraged to feel superior to the 'idol-worshipping Hindu'.

Hindus were not in a position to put the record straight, as their own elite put down Hinduism due to the malicious British education policy. Yet today, it is about time to tell the world loudly and boldly what Hinduism is about.

It is not about ruling the world. It is not about believing in unverifiable dogmas. It is not about being nice to those of one's own faith and not nice to those of other faiths.

It is about discovering what we really are, apart from the ever-changing body and mind.

The ancient rishis discovered the Oneness that underlies the apparent multiplicity, long before the Western scientists did. This conscious, blissful Oneness is not somewhere out there. It permeates everyone (and everything) and can be felt as one's essence. This essence can be called by different names, but the main thing is that **it is within everyone and within everyone's reach.**

So, we are truly all children of the same infinite divine Presence. We all belong to one big family—*Vasudhaiva Kutumbhakam.*

Yet even within a family, if some choose an adharmic lifestyle, they must be corrected. And, if they still don't mend their ways, like the Kauravas in the Mahabharata, they may need to be defeated in a war.

Chapter 22

Are Christians Under Attack in India?

THERE IS probably no other country in the world where members of other religions are as safe as in India. Hindus always gave shelter to those who were persecuted in their homelands.

Jews acknowledged that India is the only country where they were never persecuted.

Syrian Christians under their leader Thomas of Cana (Thomas the Apostle did not come to India as is commonly believed) were given refuge in the fourth century.

Parsis came in the tenth century to escape their Muslim invaders in Persia. And in 1959, some 100,000 Tibetan Buddhist refugees found shelter in India—only twelve years after the British had left India divided and poverty-stricken.

In contrast, rich USA with an area three times the size of India with only a quarter of India's population allowed one thousand Tibetan families to enter only in 1991.

Indians never hesitated to accept those who were in trouble and who wanted to preserve their faith because they did not distinguish between human beings on religious lines.

Their attitude was that all have the same Divine essence within them. For them, 'religion' is not an identity, but a natural, dharmic way of life.

So, what happened that nowadays there is a lot of talk that Christians are under attack in India? Have Hindus become intolerant?

No. Hindus have not changed. All the so-called attacks on churches which were hyped on many TV channels turned out to have been minor crimes that were unconnected with 'Hindu extremists'. In other countries, these reports would barely find space in the local paper. In India, why were they flogged for days on TV channels? Why were Christian spokesmen given plenty of airtime to falsely blame the 'Hindu Rightwingers' and claim that Christians are under attack? There seems to be an agenda by the Churches and it would need to be investigated why so many TV channels obliged.

A smashed glass pane outside one church, a fire due to a short-circuit in another church, a theft of Rs 8,000 in a convent school, stones thrown by a mixed group of Hindus and Muslim surely don't warrant hours of hyped coverage?

Yes, there was also a more serious incident: the break-in into a convent school in West Bengal, where not only Rs 1.2 million was stolen but a 72-year-old nun was gang raped.

No doubt, this was shameful, and in no time, this news reached all corners of the world. It fitted well into the image that had already been crafted since 2012—of India as a rapists' nation. The Vatican radio spoke of India's shame which went viral on the internet.

It turned out that Bangladeshi Muslims, possibly encouraged by the Pakistani secret service, were the culprits.

Typically, the media fell silent. The BBC ran a scroll that

an arrest has been made in the nun's gang rape in India. They didn't mention that he was a Bangladeshi Muslim. Neither the Vatican, nor the Cardinal, nor the Bishop apologised for their false, much-publicised pre-judgement of the case that it was connected with the Hindu's re-conversion drive of RSS (Rashtriya Swayamsevak Sangh) and VHP (Vishva Hindu Parishad).

The campaign of media and Christian representatives against 'Hindu extremists' is not likely to end soon. New incidents will keep emerging and the Christian spokesmen will again peddle the 'truth' that under Narendra Modi as Prime Minister, the Hindus are emboldened to 'attack' Christians in hate crimes and that Christians feel helpless and insecure. Some TV anchors will continue to prod them: 'Do you feel unsafe in India?' and all Christian spokesmen will again reply, 'Yes', and claim that hate crimes have increased since Modi came to power.

There are other voices, too, who do not take part in this unfair back-stabbing of their Hindu brothers and blame the Christian clergy itself for trying to sow seeds of discord between the communities. Yet those Christians, like Robert Rosario or Dr Hilda Raja, are not likely to get an invitation to represent the Christian side, because they wouldn't further the agenda of portraying Hindus in a poor light.

Mainstream media has tremendous power to shape opinions. Churches have tremendous financial and political clout. Obviously, both cooperate to portray Hindus as intolerant and hateful of other religions, contrary to facts. There is a third power that wants India to get a bad image the world over, at least as bad as its own image. It is Pakistan.

The *Sunday Guardian* of 21 March 2015 exposed that the

Pakistani secret service had increased its budget six-fold to achieve the goal that India is put into the same bracket with Pakistan on human rights issues and downgraded by the US Commission for International Religious Freedom (USCIRF).

This goal has already been achieved in projecting India as a rapist country. In the West, Pakistan, India, and Bangladesh are now being seen on the same level. In fact, India stands out negatively: it is openly thrashed for its 'anti-woman attitude', while it is politically incorrect to thrash Muslim countries. A German university professor, who quoted 'India's rape culture' as reason to reject an Indian into her course, is proof of the huge damage that this false portrayal of India has done.

Unfortunately, India did nothing to put the issue into perspective when the maligning campaign started, and it seems that India is again not doing anything to prevent an equally damaging and also false perception that Hindus are prone to hate crimes against Christians (and Muslims). Sometimes, I wonder whether Indians are even aware of how detrimental the media campaign has already been to India's image abroad.

At least the government, if not the public at large, would know that India is neither in the top league of rape countries, nor are Hindus known for hate crimes and discrimination against members of other religions.

They would know that presently, India has a population of 1,460 million, and it is unfair to compare absolute numbers of crimes with other countries. If the crimes that happen in the USA, Canada, and in all European countries including Russia plus Australia were added, then they could be compared with the number of crimes that happen in India.

Can the media be made to give a balanced reporting on the issues that it takes up?

Does anyone remember the hype that the media had created about AIDS in the 1990s? 'India is second only to South Africa' they had screamed. Nobody mentioned that India had 1,000 million and South Africa had only 50 million inhabitants. So, to be on par with South Africa, India would need to have 20 times the number of South Africa's AIDS cases. Yet it had LESS. It was at second place in ABSOLUTE numbers.

If the media were fair, they would discern that the charge of 160 hate crimes against Christians in the last 10 months, especially when those include thefts and a stone thrown by a drunkard, is no reason to shout that 'Christians don't feel safe in India'? Why do they play into the hands of the West which will be pleased to get a stick to beat India with?

In England, over 1,000 hate crimes were registered only against Jews in 2015, and over 4,000 in 2023. Proportionately, if this were to happen in India, it would mean 80,000 hate crimes in India. In USA, several Sikhs, Hindus, and Muslims were killed only because of their religion. Should the USCIRF not put the US and Europe on its watch list, before it even thinks of condemning India?

There are several indicators that clearly show that Christians are not persecuted in India and are, in fact, even pampered:

- The percentage of Christians keeps increasing.
- Their places of worship are multiplying manifold and they are free from government interference, unlike Hindu temples.
- Many Christians are in high positions.
- Missionaries have the guts to openly declare that they want to plant 100,000 churches in India and 'evangelise the whole country in this generation' (writings in a Christian youth magazine called *Blessings* in its March 2008 issue).

- Christians and other minorities are privileged and get special benefits like scholarships, etc.
- Christians can teach catechism in their schools to Christian students, while ethics teachers in those same schools must not mention Sri Krishna, or Hindu philosophy to Hindu students.

Compare this with the situation in Pakistan and it becomes evident that the 'operation equal blame' depends entirely on spreading falsehood and manipulating world opinion.

How to counter this mischievous agenda? Certainly not by going on the defensive and giving special attention to Christians. 'Justice for all, appeasement for none' is the way to go.

The nun gang rape has been carried to the eight corners of the world as a 'communal crime' because the victim was a Christian. How would the kin of a Hindu girl feel, who has been raped and killed by Muslims or Christians, but neither the media nor even the police take any interest in the case, because it is 'not communal enough' when Hindus are the victims?

Hindus have no reason to be defensive. Spokespersons are dishonest when they claim that Christians are unsafe in India. It will be difficult to find any other country where Christians who are in a minority are as safe and pampered, as they are among Hindus. If someone needs to be on the defensive, it is the Christian clergy and they know it. Maybe that is the reason why they act as bullies in tune with the dictum 'attack is the best defense'. They will stop playing the bully only when they perceive that their opponent is as strong.

Here, strength doesn't mean bullying back. It simply means to be clear, stick to the truth, and stick to dharma. It also means not to be afraid to point out the adharmic, divisive aspects of Christianity.

What is more of a hate crime: when a stone is thrown at a church by a drunkard or when respected clergy declare without any proof that Hindus are damned to eternal hellfire if they don't become members of the Church, or when they brainwash Christian children to believe this?

Christians who originally came as refugees, and later went berserk with unspeakable brutalities during the Goan Inquisition, are now on a well-planned mission with huge funds from the West to change the broad-minded attitude of Hindus from 'We ALSO revere Jesus' to a narrow-minded 'We revere ONLY Jesus'.

Contempt and intolerance for other religions is inbuilt in Christianity. Its goal is clear: all must follow Christ. Hinduism must disappear. If they say something else in Interfaith Dialogues, then that is deception. The spread of Christianity is not in India's interest. It is not in humanity's interest either.

Maybe the Prime Minister himself needs to point out on his visit to Europe that Christian Churches are on a massive conversion spree in India because they have this baseless notion that otherwise Hindus will go to hell. They should relax. Hindus won't go to hell. Most Europeans (except for those employed by the Churches) will agree with him.

However, the media campaign 'Christians are under attack' has already done a lot of damage. I just checked with a cousin in Germany. Yes, he had already heard that there were attacks on Christians in India....

Chapter 23

My Letter to Pope Francis

POPE FRANCIS *passed away on 2 April 2025. His pontificate had started in March 2013 and initially, he was getting a lot of praise for his 'bold statements'. However, he only spoke about 'respectful coexistence of religions'. He didn't walk his talk and stop conversions. In December 2013, while driving from Chennai to Puducherry, I noticed many new churches lining the highway. That's when I had the idea to write a letter to the Pope and remind him of what he said, but didn't do.*

Respected Holy Father,

Great hope for a positive change in the Catholic Church is pinned on your Pontificate and recent statements indicate that this hope may not be misplaced. **Your Holiness said in November 2013, 'The future is in the respectful coexistence of diversity and in the fundamental right to religious freedom in all its dimensions, and not in muting the different voices of religion.'**

This statement makes eminent sense and would need to be implemented by all who presently do not subscribe to a respectful coexistence of diversity regarding religions.

However, I sense (wrongly maybe) that it is a plea for other religions to respect Christianity, rather than a commitment by the Church to respect other religions. To be precise, since Christians are frequently persecuted in Islamic countries, it seems to be an appeal to 'live and let live' between the two biggest religions on earth.

Your Holiness is aware that both, Christianity and Islam, claim to be the only true religion and their God and Allah respectively, alone are true. Both religions further hold that all people on earth have to accept this claim and join their particular religion to be saved and reach heaven or paradise. Both give a serious warning to those who do not join: they will land up eternally in hell.

These claims of exclusiveness are made without any evidence whatsoever, and they even contradict each other, as both cannot be true. They require blind belief, and as blind, unreasonable belief is not natural for human beings, for many centuries it was enforced with state power and indoctrinated right from childhood with the fear of hell as the boogeyman.

May I ask Your Holiness to ponder how the respectful coexistence of diversity and the fundamental right to religious freedom is possible as long as these claims of exclusiveness are in place? Were these claims originally made to gain political power or were they made in the interest of the spiritual welfare of humanity? And may I also ask, whether Your Holiness personally believes in these claims?

I trust that privately, Your Holiness does not believe in them, as German media reported your statement that good atheists also will be redeemed. In other words, they won't go automatically to hell if they are good people who follow their conscience. However, the Vatican took pains to clarify that Your Holiness did not mean what he said. Even my mother, 95, and a staunch

Catholic all her life, expressed dismay that a perfectly sensible statement by the Pope was watered down by Vatican spokesmen.

Your Holiness may feel compelled for worldly reasons to stick to the claim of exclusiveness as dropping it would entail wrapping up all conversion attempts and, in the process, lose power, wealth, and influence. Further, there may be fear that other Christian denominations will not go along and will gain advantage over the Catholic Church. Still another worry may be that Islam will not drop the claim of exclusiveness and will push aggressively for conversion.

However, the Catholic Church was the first institution to put up this baseless claim of 'all must become Christians', which has brought unspeakable disaster upon humankind.

From this claim, the Church derived not only the 'right' but the 'duty' to storm across the globe and forcefully impose her 'belief system'—in Europe, in the Americas, and in Africa and now in Asia. It was no doubt an ingenious ploy to claim that God wants everyone to become Christian. Mark Twain famously said, 'Religion was born when the first con-man met the first fool'. I would like to change it to, 'Dogmatic religion was born when the first con-man met the first fool'.

Some centuries later, Islam followed suit, claiming that Allah wants everyone to accept Islam, and we all know the violent conflicts resulting from those unsubstantiated claims. Since the Catholic Church started this disastrous trend, she needs to reverse it. The welfare of humanity as a whole has to be the concern and not the welfare of a religious institution. Hopefully, Your Holiness has the courage to make a real, clear change for the better and will not fall for hair-splitting theological arguments, like 'redemption is possible but not salvation', etc.

Most Christians especially in Europe do not believe

anymore in unreasonable claims. The sad thing is that together with the dogmas, many reject belief in God altogether. They have not learnt to listen to their conscience and to enquire into truth, as the Church has played the role of the conscience —and truth-keeper for too long. The consequences for our societies are there for everyone to see.

However, many Christians start pondering and believe in a 'great power', but not in the Christian God. For example, when I asked some fifty Christians in Germany whether they believe that Hindus who heard about Jesus Christ, but do not convert, will go to hell, nobody said yes. Even a priest said no. And not a single German I met was in favour of missionary activity in India. Yet, Pope John Paul II declared in India in 1999 the intention of the Church to plant the cross in Asia in the new millennium and considered India as a field for a rich harvest, which goes completely against 'respectful coexistence'.

I have lived in India for the last 33 years and can assert with full confidence that India has no need of Christian missionaries, and yet huge sums of money are being pumped in to lure converts with material benefits and to build churches. I am aware that Your Holiness is responsible only for Catholics and not for the myriad of other Christian denominations that prey on poor Hindus, but if the Catholic Church made a start of truly respecting Hindus, it would have a big impact.

Maybe Your Holiness is under the impression that Hinduism is a depraved religion and Hindus would do well to accept the Christian God instead of their multiple gods. Such an impression would be completely wrong. There is no other religion that is—unjustly—denigrated as badly as Hinduism. Sorry to say that Christian (including Catholic) missionaries are in the forefront of this vilification campaign.

Only few people in the West know how profound India's ancient tradition is. A solid philosophical basis for our existence and helpful tenets for a fulfilling, meaningful life had been known in India long before 'religions', as we know them today, came into being.

The only addition Christianity brought in anew, are unverifiable dogmas that cannot possibly have a bearing on the Absolute Truth. Can an event in history impact the Absolute Truth? Will Truth make a distinction between people who are baptised and those who are not? 'There is no salvation outside the Church' is, and I may be excused for using strong language, ridiculous.

The Indian rishis had discovered ages ago that an all-pervading Presence is at the core of this universe, indescribable, but best described as absolute Consciousness. Further, the Hindu law of *Karma* preceded the Christian dictum 'as you sow so you reap'. A Council in Constantinople in 553 CE stopped Christians from believing in rebirth which would explain many riddles that trouble them, for example, why is there great injustice at birth?

The advantage of having a perfect person as a friend and guide on the spiritual path was known in India, but till some 2000 years ago nobody claimed that 'only' Krishna or 'only' Ram or 'only' Buddha can lead to salvation and that whoever does not believe it, goes to hell.

'Truth is One, the wise call it by many names', the Indian rishis declared and listed different names of gods. That was at a time, when Christianity was nowhere in sight. Surely, they would have included 'God' as another name and Jesus as an *avatar*, not suspecting to be back-stabbed by followers of 'God' declaring: 'Truth is one and must be called only by one name and is fully revealed only in one book.'

The multiple Gods in Hinduism are personified powers that help to access the formless, nameless Presence that is in all of us. Christians in India are told that Hindu Gods are devils. At the same time, Christianity tries to revive (possibly inspired by Hinduism) belief in angels, as devotion for the Invisible is easier by focusing on images.

Hinduism is not a belief system. It is a knowledge system. It is a genuine enquiry into what is true about us and the world. Hindus are not required to believe anything that does not make sense and can never be verified. There is complete freedom.

Yes, most Hindus believe in rebirth, which makes sense. Most believe in an all-pervading Brahman (many other names are in use) that is also in humans. Most believe that this Divine essence can be experienced in oneself, if the person purifies herself by certain disciplines coupled with devotion. This belief is verifiable. It is not blind. There were many rishis who realised their oneness with Brahman.

In Christianity, too, there were mystics who experienced oneness with the Divine, for example, Meister Eckhart. Sadly, he was excommunicated by the Church.

Why is the Church resisting scientific insights that there is some mystery essence in everything? And why is it difficult to accept that in the long, long history of humanity, there were several, not only one, outstanding personalities who showed the way to the Truth?

Holy Father, I request you in all sincerity to be such an outstanding personality, who guides his followers on a path of expansion, and does not straitjacket them into an unbelievable belief system, which among others, demands converting Hindus to Christianity.

Your Holiness is venerated as the representative of the Highest Power in this universe by over a billion Catholics. Many of your predecessors were not worthy of this veneration. Utmost truthfulness and integrity are required. Calculations about worldly power must not come in the way.

The Catholic Church would benefit, not lose out, if it honours Truth and gives up its claim that there is no salvation outside the Church. Truth cannot be cheated; neither can it be contained in a book. Truth is what we basically are.

Hindus, whose religion is universal and all-encompassing, respect diverse traditions. They are one of the most cultured, gentle, and peace-loving people on earth who live and let live, unless greatly provoked.

Holy Father, if you are serious about respecting other religions, the claim of exclusiveness must be scrapped and Hindus who have given to the world a deep philosophy and a great culture, must be respected.

Many of us look forward to hearing truly good news from the Catholic Church under your stewardship. The main issue that plagues the Church is not whether women should be priests or whether divorcees can take Holy Communion.

The main issue is the unfounded claim of exclusiveness regarding 'salvation'. It divides humanity into us who are right and saved, versus them who are wrong and damned. Kindly drop this harmful claim and make your Pontificate truly memorable and beneficial for all humanity.

Yours Sincerely,
Maria Wirth

Posted as a registered letter to Pope Francis on 10 December 2013 from India.

Chapter 24

My Reply to an Indian Christian Politician's Tweet

DEAR SAVIO ji,

I had the pleasure to meet you at a conference and you came across as likeable, competent, and intelligent. And I had the impression, we had in common that we both grew up as Christians but realised that Hindu or Sanatana Dharma is the better option.

That's why I was surprised, if not shocked, by your tweet:

'I am a Christian by my faith but Hindu by my roots. That's me. You cannot accept this fact about me, then it is your problem, not mine.'

Most Hindus do not know the essence of the Christian faith, and you may have thought you can state this without anyone noticing? Or maybe you yourself don't know the essence??

Here the essence is, in short:

The essence of Christianity is that Christians have the right faith and will be saved and Hindus have the wrong faith and will be damned forever. And from this follows that missionaries who dedicate their lives to save Hindu souls by getting them baptised, are doing a great job.

You would know about the claim 'There is no salvation outside of the Church'. However, hopefully, you won't take this claim seriously. I assume, for you 'Christian faith' means seeing Jesus Christ as your guide and object of devotion, as Hindus are devoted to Krishna, Ram, Shiva, Devi....

To feel devotion for Jesus is of course fine. No Hindu has any objection. They would see you as belonging to Sanatana Dharma, which accepts many ways to connect with the ultimate Cause of our existence, whom the Vedas call Brahman or Tat. But to declare devotion for Jesus as 'Christian faith' is not honest, because it is not true. Other conditions apply.

You would know that, as a Christian, you do not have the option to pick and choose. You must accept the whole doctrine of the 'faith' which, in your childhood, you may have repeated in Sunday mass umpteen times, and this doctrine postulates the exclusivity of the 'one Lord Jesus Christ, the only son of God.... For us men and our salvation, he came down from heaven...' (Nicene Creed)

So, you owe an explanation to Hindus what you mean by 'I am Christian by my faith'.

If an amiable and influential person like you, stands openly by his Christian faith, without any clarification, it will confirm Hindus in their wrong belief, that all religions are the same, and it's only some Church members, who misunderstand their religion and give trouble to Hindus and that not certain tenets of the religion itself are responsible.

The problem is precisely with the doctrine that 'there is no salvation outside of the Church'.

Please do clarify in a public post, whether you agree with this crucial tenet that there is no salvation outside of the

Church and that, by extension, missionaries do a good job.

Yes, most missionaries really believe that they do a great job. They did not get out of their brainwashing. But I am sure, you do not believe this any longer. But please… say it openly. You owe it to Hindus.

And hopefully you won't mind my plain speak….

Regards
Maria

Chapter 25

An NRI who Converted to Christianity

ONCE ON a flight from Germany to India, one of those bright, young Indians sat across the aisle. We started talking. He was a science lecturer at an American university.

When food came, he ordered non-veg and I ordered, veg. I teasingly asked, 'Non-veg'? He replied, 'Yes, I started eating meat when I converted to Christianity eight years ago.'

'You… converted… to… Christianity?' I asked in disbelief. 'How could you do this? Are you not aware of their doctrine?' I kept throwing questions at him. Surely, he had not expected this reaction from a white woman with the name Maria. In all likelihood, he had converted because he wanted to belong and fit into the new surroundings in America. And, in all likelihood, there was also some friendly nudging from missionaries to come for mass and lunch afterwards….

But since I grew up as a Christian, I knew what Christianity claims, and he didn't have the answers. As most Christians do, he fell back at the 'personal experience with Jesus' which convinced him that Christianity is the true religion.

I told him, 'If your trust in Jesus helps you, great, but why convert?' Doesn't your own tradition stress the importance of devotion and does it hinder you from trusting Jesus?' And, while for you, Jesus may be the ideal guide, for others it may be Shiva or Krishna or Devi. Your tradition allows you freedom whereas the Church binds you to the doctrine. For example, it claims that Hindus go to hell. Do you believe that your Hindu brothers and sisters will go to hell?' I asked.

I couldn't believe his answer and by now, he did not look so bright to me. He said, 'Yes, we have to believe this.' … Do we have to?

So, I asked him about his family. 'Will they burn in hell?' He had managed to convince his parents to convert, but his siblings had not (yet) converted.

I felt pity for him. His mental freedom to question and to enquire was gone, and I hope he will get out of it again.

Chapter 26

Are There a Good Reason to Accept Christianity?

THIS WAS *a question on Quora to which I had replied. While writing this chapter, I have modified and expanded my original reply.*

If you have not been born into a Christian family and have not been baptised, there is absolutely no good reason for you to accept the Christian religion. And, if you have been baptised, you should reflect on what is helpful in your belief, and what is harmful for you, and for humanity as a whole.

Let me explain: I was born into a Christian family and the belief in a great God, who knows and loves me, was helpful for me as a child. My mother taught me a short prayer which rhymed in German. It was nice to repeat, and it meant:

'Dear God, I am small, my heart is pure, let me be fully your own.'

It created intimacy with God, and I felt protected by his greatness.

Soon, I was also taught about Jesus being the only son of God, who died for our sins, and rose from the dead, and other such beliefs. I was also taught about hell. For example: if I don't go to church on Sunday, and I don't confess this sin to the priest, I will be thrown into eternal hellfire.

This was harmful for me because I became very timid, and I believed something which was not true.

Later in school, another harmful aspect was taught: Christianity alone has the full truth. All those heathens, who don't accept Christ as their saviour, will burn eternally in hell.

This claim, made without any proof, also cannot be true. Moreover, it is clearly harmful for humanity. It makes Christians arrogant. Naturally, they look down on those heathens who are 'damned'. And, over the centuries, how easily they have even killed them! The Church has left a very bloody trail on earth, and all this in the name of a 'loving God'.

Now let's look at the beneficial aspect of Christianity: it is the belief in God, in a Supreme Being, who is more powerful than humans.

Yet to believe in a Supreme Being, there is no need to convert to Christianity. This belief is natural. It makes sense. It is ancient. It was there much before Christ had walked on earth.

In the Vedas, Brahman is the eternal, infinite Consciousness that is the essence in all. This essence is Sat-Chit-Ananda (Truth-Consciousness-Bliss), and it is the same in everyone. Only the names and forms are different, and temporary.

Now, if one compares Brahman with the Christian God, it becomes clear that the Christian God is a distortion of Brahman. The Christian God is not the essence in all, but is separate from His creation. Moreover, He loves only those who believe in the Bible, and sends the rest to hell forever.

It's easy to see which view is closer to Truth and more

beneficial for humanity, and it is no surprise that the Indian texts are full of universal prayers: 'May all be happy', 'Lead us (all) from untruth to Truth, from darkness to light....'

In contrast, when Christians pray for others, they pray that those who are not yet Christians, may get baptised and join their club.

So, despite growing up as a Christian, I could see that the Hindu view is closer to the truth and therefore, when someone asks me if I am Christian, I answer that I am Hindu.

Hindus don't proselytise. They don't try to increase their numbers, unlike Christianity and Islam. Actually, I wished they would make an effort to spread their eternal wisdom and make people see sense.

The world would be a better place.

Yet, a question remains, when there is no good reason for converting, why do so many Hindus convert? The main reason is (and it is not a good reason) that the poor are given material benefits, like lower school fees or outright money, and the rich expect social benefits, since powerful personalities, like Sonia Gandhi, are Christians. The NRI mentioned in the previous chapter probably also expected to fit in better with his American friends.

Unfortunately, the poor are also deceived by so-called 'proofs' that the Christian God is more powerful than the Hindu Gods. I heard an example from the backwater area of Kerala: A missionary had an idol of Sri Krishna and another one of Jesus on a (wooden) cross. He threw both into water and lo and behold, Jesus floated while Krishna sank.

A Tibetan, who used to be in a Christian boarding school in Northern India, told me this example—the children were asked to pray to Buddha before sleeping. Nothing special happened. Next night, they were asked to pray to Jesus, and lo and behold, the next morning they found toffees near their pillows.

Another method of missionaries is to frighten people that the world will end soon, and if one does not belong to the true faith, one will burn in hell forever. Once in Mussoorie, I was handed a booklet with exactly this claim by the missionaries. On the last page, the reader was urged to hurry up, and quickly get in contact with the given address and convert in time, to be saved from eternal hellfire.

Chapter 27

Are Jihadis to Blame for Attacking Us?

I WROTE the following article in 2016, after a terror attack in a Christmas market in Berlin. Not much has changed since then. Terror attacks are still being perpetrated by Muslim migrants on German citizens; for example, in December 2024, a Muslim struck again by driving a car into a Christmas market killing six people and injuring over 60. Two months later, in February 2025, a migrant drove a car into an election rally in Munich, killing two, including a 2-year-old girl, and injuring over 30.

The fear of lone-wolf-attacks has changed the atmosphere in Europe. Women feel insecure while walking alone, and even men are not keen to go out alone at night. The security business is booming. Pepper sprays and other articles for self-defence are in great demand. More security, more police is seen as the solution to a problem which has not been well-analysed.

Apart from the many knife attacks, there is now the fear of cars or trucks being used to create terror, as it happened at the Christmas market in Berlin in 2016. A Tunisian migrant drove a truck into the milling crowd, killing 12 and injuring 56.

On a memorial for the victims of this terror attack, the German Chancellor placed a white rose below a board which asked in big letters: *'Warum?'* This 'Why' naturally haunts good-natured, naïve Germans who welcomed the refugees and volunteered in refugee shelters when they first came into the country.

Yet, inexcusably, this 'Why' also seems to haunt many of the political class. Chancellor Merkel considered the attack as 'incomprehensible'. It seemed she and her government had no clue why certain people turned against their German hosts when they had been so generous. But how can they defeat Islamist terrorism, when they don't know what motivates the terrorists?

For the last few decades, Europeans have been sold on a wonderful world, where we all live happily together as global citizens irrespective of race, gender, religion, and nationality. Sweden was at the forefront of this movement. In a TV clip, children from Sweden, Africa, and Asia sang a song about how Sweden belongs to all of them and how wonderful it is to love each other, merrily dancing around holding hands.

No doubt, a 'liberal world order' where all human beings irrespective of differences are respected, is a worthy idea. Donald Trump has been demonised for not endorsing it and is seen as the greatest danger to such an idea. Angela Merkel reminded him, perhaps a bit too self-righteously, of those liberal values when she congratulated him for winning the US election in 2016.

Yet, whoever has eyes to see, knows that the reality is the stark opposite of a wonderful, liberal world. The huge influx of 'refugees' did not make things better for Europe, as was heralded. It made things infinitely worse. Meanwhile, since the situation has gone so much out of hand with crime-rates sky-rocketing and the fear of terror attacks all-pervasive, the liberal elite felt compelled to explain what went wrong. Unfortunately, either they are dishonest—or plain ignorant.

They explained: 'The New World Order (NWO) does not come without a cultural change. Yet, instead of embracing multi-culturalism, the natives resist it. They are suspicious of 'the other'. They want to stick to their old way of life, and that is why we now have a big problem because the nationalist, extremist right-wing is gaining ground. This is most unfortunate.'

They don't call it only unfortunate. They label the right-wingers as fascists, Nazis, xenophobics, Islamophobics, and openly spew hatred against them, all the while claiming that they, the 'liberals', only want all to love each other.

If someone asks whether the newcomers to Europe even WANT a liberal world, he is shouted down. Never blame the migrants, is the motto, and never ever claim that religion may be the cause why 'happily living together' does not work.

To be precise: never mention Islam. Nowadays, one can malign Christianity and of course Hinduism, but Islam is out-of-bounds. To bring in Islam as a possible cause for friction is forbidden, so much so, that in our 'liberal' societies, there is a risk of ending up in jail.

Why is it so? Why do liberals close their eyes to the fact that Islam is not liberal? Neither is Christianity. Nor do these two religions hide it. Both insist that their followers must 'religiously' stick to the doctrines if they don't want to burn in hell forever.

Now, how to establish a liberal world when about half the world's population is indoctrinated to believe that all humanity needs to follow a particular book before peace can descend on earth? It is even more complicated: about a quarter of the population is told that God wants all to follow the Bible and Jesus, and another quarter is told that Allah wants all to follow the Quran and Mohammed.

Whether Jesus or Mohammed had intended this narrow-minded interpretation is not the question. It is also not the question whether there are verses in those books which contradict this narrow view. The problem is that this narrow interpretation has been indoctrinated by the clergy into children since over a thousand years with terrible effects and nobody is stopping it.

Wolfgang Trusheim, of Frankfurt's State Security office, gave a worrying account:

'This is about war, about children being indoctrinated. They are only in primary school and already they fantasise about how, when they grow up, they want to join the *Jihad* and kill infidels. They say: 'I'm not allowed to play football with you, but when I grow up, I will kill you, because you are an infidel."[6]

There was a clip on YouTube about a religious class for Muslim boys in a German school. The teacher spoke in broken German and kept repeating to the 6 to 10-year-olds that they must not make friends with German boys, because those boys are bad, and will be sent to hell by Allah.

---

6 https://www.gatestoneinstitute.org/9614/germany-saudi-arabia-qatar-kuwait

Is it then a surprise that a 12-year-old Muslim boy tried to plant a bomb in a Christmas market in Southern Germany soon after the attack in Berlin? The question is: can he be blamed for wanting to kill kafirs? And if he can't be blamed, then can he be blamed when he is 17 or 20?

How are children supposed to get out of the brainwashing, when their surrounding endorses the claim that Allah likes Muslims but hates non-Muslims (kafirs)? This when even respected leaders, like the first education minister in Independent India, Maulana Abdul Kalam Azad, had not got out of such brainwashing? Or else, would he have exhorted Muslims to join Jihad for a pan-Islamic Caliphate?

A very crucial tenet of both Islam and Christianity is that a human being has only one life. Belief in rebirth was banned for Christians in a Council in Constantinople in 553 AD, long before Islam was born. This 'one life only' has an advantage for those religions: the fear of eternal hell prevents their followers from relaxing and experimenting. And both religions make sure that the fear of hell seeps deeply into the psyche of children.

Hindus and others, who do not go through this indoctrination, can't even imagine that the fear of hell can be real, but it is.

Once, I received a mail from a 38-year-old American who wrote that my articles helped him a lot in seeing things more clearly, but sometimes he still worries: 'What if the Church is right, and eternal hell is true?'

This question often haunts lukewarm Christians and surely also Muslims, and makes their life miserable and guilt-ridden. Even a moderate sounding outfit like the Centre for Peace and Spirituality (CPS), founded by Maulana Wahiduddin Khan, preaches this basic tenet in its 'Quranic wisdom':

'According to the Quran, a person's life has been divided into two phases: the pre-death and the post-death period. The present life is only temporary and is meant as a test. Depending upon our performance in this test, we shall be judged in the eternal life after death. The Quran aims to make one aware of this reality and to help one lead one's life in this world in such a way that one is rewarded with Paradise in the life hereafter.'

Reading the Quran, one clearly gets the impression that paradise is only for true Muslims, not for the hypocrites among them and, of course, not for kafirs. What is expected from a true Muslim?

Quran 61.10/11 says that two things are expected: One is faith in Allah and his Prophet, and two, doing one's utmost for jihad with one's person and wealth.

A *jihadi* is promised a higher status in paradise (Quran 4.95). Is it a surprise that especially criminals, join jihad to 'redeem' themselves? Should they be called monsters or should they be congratulated for wanting to wash themselves off their sins by doing what they (wrongly) understand as the wish of the Supreme Being?

Clearly, something has been very badly misunderstood. Is it not the responsibility of the elders to point this out and save not only the potential victims of future terror attacks but also the Muslim youth?

Hindus and Buddhists, especially need to challenge this wrong understanding. How can they 'respect' it only because 'religion' is attached to it? Why is Islam treated like a protected species?

Does 'The right to religious freedom' mean the right to Islamise the world? Does it mean the right to Christianise the world? Do Hindus have the right to stay Hindus? When the right to freedom of religion is given to a religion, like Christianity and Islam, whose final goal is obliteration of all other religions, does it not obliterate the rights of other religions?

Is it necessary to respect the claim that a book has been divinely revealed, even if it contains hate speech?

Since there are several books from different religions which all claim to be the divinely revealed truth and which contradict each other, how can those claims be taken at face value and be protected by law? Should there not be a genuine, open-minded debate on what does Truth actually constitute??

Many questions, which hardly anyone asks—not even those who framed the right to religious freedom in international bodies like the United Nations.

We are faced with a big problem due to divergent and implausible religious views:

A young jihadi is convinced that killing kafirs is the right thing to do as it pleases Allah who wants only Muslims in the world.

A young Christian missionary is convinced that '*bringing the light of Christ to those who wallow in darkness*' by hook or by crook is the right thing to do, as Jesus wants all people to be baptised.

Yet ultimately, both, the jihadi and the missionary are pawns in a cynical power game. They are convenient foot soldiers. Did not the Deep State via CIA encourage students (Taliban) to become radical Islamists? Why? Because it wanted them to ferociously fight the Soviets as a Holy war—in its own interest of course.

Once children are 'taught' the wrong truth, it is not easy to get it out from their system even when they are grown up. Their identity is intimately connected with what they believe, and often reason cannot break through their natural impulse to defend their identity, especially when people in their surroundings share the same beliefs.

It needs an open environment, where questions can be asked fearlessly, where sensible answers are given, and where holy books are not untouchable. A good start would be a debate on whether there is only one life or whether rebirth is more likely. Why is there injustice in the world? Why are some born to caring parents and others to abusive drunkards?

Research into rebirth, with over 3,000 cases in the archives of Virginia University, also supports the view that everybody gets many lives on this appearance level of human existence. If the Supreme Being really wanted all to be Christians or Muslims, why would He give to some the advantage of being born in a Christian or Muslim family and yet deny that privilege to others?

How can the Creator of all be so cruel to damn us to excruciating pain in hellfire for billion trillion years after a few years of life where our only fault was that we called out to the Supreme by a different name, but in our hearts, we were great believers in a Supreme Power?

Humanity would gain greatly if such topics would be debated in an open atmosphere. Truth would be honoured. Trust in 'the other' would come back. A liberal, plural world would be possible.

Only some hard-line clerics might lose out. And the 'liberals' in the media with their soft corner for illiberal ideologies would probably rush to the defence of those hard-line clerics….

Chapter 28

An Interview with a Would-be Jihadi

POLITICIANS AND media worldwide maintain that jihadis are 'misguided youths' but don't seem to be interested to know who or what misguides them.

On the other hand, those who joined ISIS are clear: 'We follow the true Islam', they declare with full conviction and ridicule those who think otherwise.

Killing people, who go peacefully about their daily lives, clearly goes against human nature. So why do jihadis do it? Apart from some pathological cases, the reason is that they are convinced that they are doing the right thing. Of course, these youths are misguided, but by whom or what?

To be fair—the jihadis are not the first to be misguided. Communists were misguided by a divisive ideology, which made them believe that if certain people were dead, a glorious future would await them.

Christians were misguided by their baseless belief that heathen and heretics are an eyesore to their God and are better done away with if they refuse to join the 'true faith'. Thanks to the pressure of a more enlightened civil society, a couple of centuries ago, they had to give up torturing and killing in the name of God.

Islamic terror is one of the biggest threats that our world is facing today and has been facing for over 1000 years. So, it is of utmost importance to understand what drives the jihadis. The German *SZ-Magazin* carried an eye-opening interview with a would-be ISIS-jihadi that gives insight into their mind-set[7].

It is about Erhan, a Turkish origin, almost shy youth of 22 years. Some of his friends were in Syria. He tried to join them but didn't succeed. A few years ago, he became dissatisfied with the lukewarm "Euro-fake" Islam that his parents practised in Germany. His father didn't even pray. He wanted to follow the 'real' Islam and started reading the Quran. He grew a beard, prayed five times a day, went to the mosque, and even wore a turban to school. His classmates asked him what happened, and he told them about the Quran. They never asked him again. 'I had expected more criticism from them,' Erhan said.

His friends and he were banned from the local mosques in their Bavarian town because they kept lecturing the Muslims there that they don't follow the Quran correctly. However, the ban convinced them that they were on the right path, because 'in the Quran it is written that there will be opposition'.

Erhan was convinced that Islam is the only true religion, and he wanted ISIS to create a state where 'the Quran is

---

7   http://sz-magazin.sueddeutsche.de/texte/anzeigen/42259/Ich-glaub-das-steht-irgend-wo-im-Koran

lived as Allah wants it'. When the interviewer reminded him of ISIS's brutality, he replied, 'If one kills for a good cause, it is legitimate'.

One of Erhan's friends died fighting in Aleppo. 'Were you sad?' he was asked. 'At first a little, but I also envied him, because I know where he is,' he replied, but strongly rebuked the notion that it is because of the virgins. 'If only women were to be gained, I would not do it. I do it for Allah.'

He comes across as a naïve young man who wanted to make his life meaningful and found guidance in the Quran. He connected with like-minded youths. They checked out several groups and were convinced that ISIS was the best to join because its goal was clearly in tune with the Quran: the goal to spread the Islamic State till the whole world is for Allah.

'Oh believers, fight them until there is no more mischief and the *Deen* of Allah (way of life prescribed by Allah) is established completely.' (Quran 8.39)

'Oh believers, fighting has been made obligatory for you much to your dislike. It is quite possible that what you dislike is good for you.... Allah knows and you do not.' (Quran 2.216)

'Those believers who stay at home—having no physical disabilities—are not equal to those who make jihad in the cause of Allah with their wealth and person. Allah has granted a higher rank to those who make jihad.... They have special higher ranks, forgiveness, and mercy. Allah is forgiving, merciful.' (Quran 4.95/6)

Could Erhan and his friends have any doubt about what these passages mean? Does it need an 'Islam expert' to interpret them? If the experts had come to the conclusion that those passages were meant exclusively for the contemporaries of Mohammed and not for all time thereafter, they should have said this loud and clear long ago—too much blood has been shed over the last fourteen centuries, much of it in India. But those experts kept quiet. Does it follow that the Quran exhorts Muslims to fight till the *Deen* of Allah is established?

The command to fight the enemy appeals to young men. Islam is far more successful than Christianity in making men stand by their religion.

A German police study which questioned 45,000 students between fourteen and sixteen years of age, about their level of religiosity and their readiness to be violent, confirmed this:

Girls were more religious than boys in all religions except in Islam. Further, those who considered themselves 'more religious' were less inclined to be violent in all religions, except in Islam.

Small boys everywhere like toy guns. Bigger boys need a good reason to fight. A Divine command to fight those who are evil, is the perfect reason for many youngsters to fight. Further, there is the 'divine promise' that it will be a win-win situation: if one dies, one is guaranteed to enjoy paradise, and if one lives, one benefits from the wealth and the women of those killed.

There are many passages in the Quran where the unbelievers are portrayed as most despicable, for whom perdition and eternal hellfire are certain. For example Quran 98.6 says, 'Surely those who disbelieve from among the people of the Book and the *Mushrikin* (idolaters) shall be in fire of hell, to dwell therein forever. They are the worst of all creatures.'

Even the torture in hell is described in horrific details. Quran 22.19-22 says: 'As for the disbelievers, garments of fire will be cut out for them, boiling water will be poured over their heads which will not only melt their skins but also the inner parts of their bellies, and there will be maces of iron to lash them. Whenever in their anguish they try to escape therefrom, they will be forced back therein, and will be told, 'Taste the punishment of conflagration'.'

Do such passages explain the savagery of ISIS? Have the vivid images of hell over the centuries instigated the brutalities of the Christian Inquisition and of the Muslim invaders in India and elsewhere? Was there such brutality against civilians before the arrival of religions which claimed 'eternal hellfire for disbelievers'?

It is difficult to see the ruthless terrorist in Erhan. But he may turn out to become just that—a ruthless killer. He said that he would even kill his parents if they opposed the Islamic State. He is sure that 'In 20, 30 years the Islamic State will be in Germany and it will gradually cover the whole planet'.

Are we not responsible to stop these youngsters from destroying themselves and others? Yet, is it possible as long as those passages are considered the word of Allah? Even if ISIS gets defeated, new terror groups will continue to draw legitimacy from those passages, and ultra rich powerbrokers in suits and ties behind the scenes will instigate youngsters for their own interests, making them believe that Allah will be pleased, if they blow themselves up killing kafirs in the process. Those passages have tremendous potential in mobilising youngsters for a cause that in their eyes, is worthwhile and just. They don't realise that they are being used—like the US used the Taliban to fight the Russians in Afghanistan.

Erhan's parents in Germany, his uncle in Turkey, and even the Imam of the local mosque tried to prevent him from turning radical. But what can they tell him? That he should not take the Quran seriously? That Allah didn't mean what he said? Erhan considers those Imams who are against ISIS as old, confused men. And he has a point, but it could also make him wonder why older Muslims, including Imams, do not opt to become suicide bombers even if they have a serious illness. Are they not convinced that paradise is guaranteed by killing others?

'What can stop you?' the journalist had asked Erhan.

His answer: 'Nobody can stop me.'

He is right. No outsider can stop him. If a Muslim tries to influence him, he will see him as a hypocrite. And if an unbeliever tries to influence him, he is sure that he only wants him to leave 'the right path'.

But there is one thing that can stop him: it is doubt.

Once doubt springs up, it is not possible to regain the former strong beliefs. I know this from my own experience, as I also once believed in eternal hell.

If Erhan starts wondering whether the compassionate Allah really wants all this killing, he could come out of the grip of his blind belief.

Chapter 29

My letter to Zakir Naik

THIS LETTER is one of my most read articles. I had also put it on Quora, from where it was removed after 17 hours, under the pretext that it violated its plagiarism rule. Plagiarism? My own article? I had mentioned that this is my article from my blog, had also given the link. I can only guess that, maybe, I should have put the whole thing in quotation marks…

Zakir Naik had once told his Muslim audience that they can easily convert Hindus. They only needed to show Hindus a picture of Lord Ganesha, with his elephant head and big belly, and ask them whether this is the God they worship.

He threw a challenge to prove that Ganesha (also called Ganapati) is God.

Someone commented on my blog, 'We Hindus are pathetic. We just complain about feeling insulted, but we don't counter him.'

This comment struck me. But who was I to counter? Some Hindu representative should do it… But probably neither the Gurus, nor the Swamis were doing it. Generally, they don't criticise other religions in spite of the fact that Christian and Islamic clergy *not only criticise, but also badly demean Hinduism. Zakir Naik is only one example.*

Do Hindus even know what is preached in the innumerable churches and mosques across India? I know for sure that Hindu Gods are called devils by the Christian clergy. Yet strangely, Hindus neither explain their faith nor challenge the dogmas of Christianity and Islam, even though they have a solid philosophical base for their beliefs, which lacks in those two dogmatic religions. Both depend fully on blind belief.

So, I sat down to reply to his challenge.

Namaste Dr Zakir Naik,

You challenged to prove that Ganapati is God.

I assume you mean by God the Supreme Being that Muslims call Allah.

Now what do we know about Allah?

Foremost, Allah is great and merciful, and the faithful as well as the unfaithful are loudly reminded of it five times a day. He also knows what all human beings are doing, but is separate from them. It is claimed that Allah has communicated his final words to Prophet Mohammed. Those words are in the Quran. Allah declared that Islam alone is true. So, all human beings must follow Islam because other paths are wrong. And they must hurry up, because every human being has only one life.

Those, who do not accept Islam during their lifetime, will be thrown into eternal hellfire where 'boiling water will be poured over their heads that not only melts their skin but also the inner parts of their bellies…' (Quran 22.19-22)

Clearly, here is where Allah's mercy ends. He does not brook any dissent. And, Al-Fatiha 1 in the Quran, which starts compassionately, ends with: 'Oh Allah, guide us to the

Right Way. The Way of those whom You have favoured, not of those who have earned Your wrath....'

This means, Allah is merciful only to his followers who are called Muslims and he is wrathful to those who are not Muslims.

Dr Zakir Naik, I am confident that I got the concept of 'God' in Islam right because Christianity has a similar concept. And I dare to claim that it is not true. Can you prove (and this challenge also goes to Christian clerics) that Allah/God is indeed so unfair and divisive? Can you prove there will be this huge cauldron of fire where billions of people will burn for ever after Judgment Day? Do these claims of 'eternal hellfire for unbelievers' not rather have the purpose to keep the flock in check? To divide and rule?

There are about two billion Christians, who are told they have to remain Christians, otherwise they can't go to heaven. And then there are about 2 billion Muslims who are told that they have to remain Muslims, otherwise they can't go to paradise. Both religions had plenty of time to sort out which one is true, but they did not do it.

Why? Because they cannot prove it. They can only make claims and counterclaims and fight among themselves, between Muslims and Christians and with heathens or infidels. They do this for the last 2,000 years.

Under these circumstances, can anyone claim that Islam or Christianity is beneficial for humanity? Is it not time to have a thorough check of what REALLY is the truth?

In regard to the Absolute Truth, Dr Zakir Naik, your ancestors, the Indian rishis, made valuable contributions and you can be proud of them. In ancient times, long, long before Christianity or Islam appeared on the scene, the rishis had a very mature understanding of Brahman which would be 'Absolute Truth' or 'Supreme Being' or 'God' in English.

Brahman is not personal, not a superhuman entity somewhere in heaven, not male or female, not jealous of other gods, not revengeful if ignored, but is Sat-Chit-Ananda, the conscious, One Essence in all names and forms—like the one ocean is the essence in all the waves.

The rishis realised that this universe is a wrong perception of Brahman. They called it Maya, not really true, more like a simulation.

The *Tripura Rahasya* declares that for anything to qualify as Absolute Truth, it has to be always—past, present and future—and it has to be self-evident.

The rishis came to the conclusion that nothing fulfils these criteria except pure (= thought-free) consciousness. This consciousness is here and now, always, everywhere. Yet we miss it because we focus only on things or thoughts, emotions, etc.— like, when we focus a torchlight in a room only on the furniture and miss the empty space. Infinite space, which throbs with life and love is actually a good metaphor for Sat-Chit-Ananda—the highest truth that underlies names and forms (*nama-rupa*).

Science has meanwhile discovered the *Sat*-aspect of the truth. Oneness is there. To discover that this Oneness is also aware (*Chit*) and blissful (*Ananda*) scientists would need to turn to their own consciousness to research further instead of looking outside. So far, the scientists do not support the claim of the rishis that this manifestation is not only one but also alive and full of bliss. But can they know for sure? No.

In one point you are right, Dr Zakir Naik: There is only one Truth, one God, which the wise call by different names. But the nature of it you got wrong. It does not send non-Muslims or non-Christians eternally into hellfire. The Supreme Being is indeed merciful and great.

But you wanted to know whether Ganapati is God.

May I explain a bit of your ancestors' tradition which struck me as most profound when I came to know of it?

Sanatana Dharma is not only about intellectually knowing about Sat-Chit-Ananda, but about realising it. Since Brahman is all pervading, it must be also in us (Upanishads declare: *Ayam Atma Brahma*). So, we can tap and feel it. For this, however, we need to follow certain rules. We need to purify ourselves, lead a moral life, speak the truth, etc. To cheat, lie, hate, etc. is not conducive for this purification. Yet one factor is very conducive: Bhakti—love for God.

Here Hindu Dharma brings in Ishwara.

The concept of Ishwara is close to the Abrahamic notion of a personal God but far more benevolent. There is no eternal hell for unbelievers. Everyone gets chance after chance in life after life till he realises that he is not a separate wave, but one with the ocean.

Ishwara is God with attributes and has innumerable aspects, as this universe has innumerable aspects or human nature has innumerable aspects. These aspects are personified in different Deities, and the devotee can choose the one who is dearest to him. It helps to develop love for the invisible Truth—for example through Ganapati.

Those Devas are misunderstood and mistakenly much maligned by the Abrahamic religions. They are not separate entities but access points to the one Brahman, which is otherwise unimaginable. It is possible to feel familiar with them, to love them, to talk to them. And the scriptures leave no doubt that Devas are ultimately only Brahman.

And here, Dr Naik, you may get an answer to your question whether Ganapati is ultimately the Supreme Being.

The *Ganapati Atharvashirsa Upanishad*, which is part of the *Atharva Veda*, states: *Tvameva kevalam karta si, tvameva kevalam dharta si, tvameva kevalam harta si.*

Tvameva sarvam khalvidam brahmasi, tvam saksadatma si nityam.

It means: You alone are the creator, you alone are the sustainer, you alone are the annihilator. All this is Brahman and you are that Brahman. You are indeed the witnessing Atma eternally.

This declaration, however, is not unique for Ganapati. It is said for other deities, too.

Yet the fact that this is written in a sacred text, is not proof enough. There are plenty of sacred texts in this world, and if everything in them is blindly accepted as true, we end up with all kinds of proclaimed truths, which are not true.

We need to verify what is declared as truth on the touchstone of reason, intuition and experience. If it contradicts all of these, it is not worth believing it and certainly not dying for it.

The proof that all deities are Brahman is, because only Brahman really exists. Brahman is like the ocean. The waves are not separate from it. The name with which one worships the Divine, does not matter. What matters is how much devotion one feels. The greater the devotion, the more miracles can happen. Ganapati is loved by millions of Hindus worldwide. He is the door through which they try to access Sat-Chit-Ananda.

Sanatana Dharma is very ancient. And yet the rishis had such deep insights, for example that the world is Maya, a wrong perception of what is really true—like seeing a snake when in fact there is only a rope. Westerners who ridiculed Hindus because they believe that the world is an illusion, keep quiet now, as science supports the Hindu view.

Great men have come and gone in India's ancient civilisation. Some have been made into Gods. There is nothing wrong with it. The Divine is in all.

It should make you reflect, Dr Naik, that science keeps validating the insights of the rishis, for example the mindboggling age of the universe, or the ultimate Oneness of all.

Attempts to vilify India's tradition by you and others are successful because the British weaned Indians away from their tradition and therefore, even many Hindus know little about it. Yet if you are sincere, you will realise that the wisdom of your ancestors scores high over the worldview and the mindset of Abrahamic religions. The attitude 'We alone are right and you go to hell if you don't accept our religion' is doing great harm to humanity. It may be helpful for world dominion, but do you want to live in a world where everyone has to wear a straitjacket?

If I were you, Dr Naik, I would be worried especially about one thing: what if you wake up after death and there is NO paradise waiting for you?

What, if all those jihadis, who were inspired by you, cursed you after realising there was no paradise for them?

What if you are taking birth again in another form and reap the fruits of your actions of this life, where you consciously or unconsciously distorted the truth?

Rebirth is not only mentioned in the Indian texts. There is also plenty of evidence for it—over 3,000 cases are documented in the archives of Virginia University.

Dr Naik, I don't know how deeply you believe what you preach. I know from personal experience how effective brainwashing in childhood can be. But I also know that it is possible to get out of it.

For me, it was a great relief to come out of the Christian religious straitjacket and I would encourage you to also genuinely enquire into the Absolute Truth. Your concept of God is not the Truth. You quote a book as support. Truth does not fit into a book. Truth is THAT WHAT TRULY IS.

Your ancestors, the Indian rishis, spoke from experience, not from book knowledge.

Yours Sincerely
Maria Wirth

Chapter 30

A Pakistani Woman's Concern for Hindus

A PAKISTANI woman, Zainab A Khan, keeps warning Hindus on Twitter (@ZainabAKhan2) that they have no chance against Muslims if they don't realise the danger they are in. She seems to be genuinely caring towards Hindus, which had an explanation in her pinned Twitter bio. It read:

'Who am I? A lawyer. Dated and married an amazing Hindu guy, who was killed by my family when he visited Pakistan after being promised a safe visit. Lost my voice after being shot but still working full time as a lawyer. This should settle this. Stop asking if I'm Muslim or Pakistani.' (Meanwhile, she changed her pinned tweet)

Once, she put out a tweet asking Hindus to understand that 'In Islam, religion is above all'.

This set me thinking. What should actually be above all? I put the question out on Twitter. The first reply to my tweet said 'Nation should be above all'.

Usually, Hindus demand from Muslims that 'nation' and 'constitution' must come first. But is it so, even for Hindus?

Spontaneously, I felt that the most important thing is to be true to oneself, having integrity, doing what feels right according to one's conscience, which basically means: following dharma.

Suppose the national authorities ask you to do something that does not feel right then what would you do? It can happen. It has happened in dictatorships.

Now, if a Hindu is convinced that it is not right and that one's Ishta Deva would not approve of doing it, would he not put dharma and his Ishta Deva first?

Dharma is often equated with religion. Does it mean, Muslims and Hindus are on the same page since they both put 'religion above all'?

Not quite.

The reason is that dharma is different from the 'religions of the book' to which all Abrahamic religions belong. These religions don't ask their followers to follow their conscience or dharma but demand that first and foremost, they follow the book.

For them, the book is the highest authority, and not their innate knowledge about what is right and wrong.

As a child, I learnt in catechism class that I must follow the Church if there is a discrepancy between my conscience and what the Church teaches.

Now, if the 'Holy Book' teaches what feels right, there is no problem. For example, both the Bible and the Quran ask their followers to believe in a Supreme Power, and fully trust it. This makes sense. They also ask to be charitable, good human beings. That is also in tune with one's conscience.

So, is there even an issue where the religions of the book are not in tune with one's conscience and if yes, would people follow it?

Probably, most people would NOT go against their conscience. For example, if a book claimed that those people, who don't believe in this book, can be treated badly and even killed, it wouldn't feel right. At least it would need some proof.

But, if people are forced to choose between being killed and following the book, most people would probably choose the book over their conscience. Once accepted, then the following generations can easily be indoctrinated right from childhood, which is very effective.

For example, every new generation of Muslim children reads in Quran 2.116: 'Fighting has been made obligatory for you, much to your dislike. It is quite possible that something, which you don't like, is good for you, and that something which you love is bad for you. Allah knows and you don't.'

Blind, unverifiable belief is not natural for humans.

This indoctrination has been going on ever since the dogmatic religions have been founded. They insist on blind belief, yet belief, which cannot be verified, is not natural for human beings who have been given intelligence.

There is a big difference between verifiable and unverifiable beliefs.

Let's give an example of a verifiable belief: Suppose, you live in Delhi and you don't know about the ocean. Somebody tells you that if you travel continuously southwards, you will reach a vast expanse of water. Now, if you consider the person trustworthy, you may believe it and start travelling south. With persistence, you will realise that what he said was true.

But someone else may not believe that such a vast expanse of water is possible and therefore, will never see the ocean. Or, someone else may start travelling, but when he reaches Bhopal, and there is still no ocean, he might even unfairly call the person a fraud.

Similarly, the wisdom of the rishis also needs to be first believed. Then, steps need to be taken to experience the truth of what they said.

On the other hand, the belief that 'Jesus saved humanity from the original sin through his death' or that 'Prophet Mohammed was told the final truth by the Archangel Gabriel', can never be verified. It will always remain only 'belief'.

How can we convince the followers of the religions of the book, that we humans have an inbuilt capacity to know what is right and wrong, and that it needs to be heeded?

Most of us feel that we must have come from the same Source and we must have a right to be here on earth.

Most of us know that it's wrong to purposely harm others, who did not harm us.

Most of us know that being helpful and compassionate is better than being selfish and cruel. And in situations, where we are not sure what is right, we should take inspiration from the scriptures or advice from worthy people, but the advice needs to make sense and feel right.

A US based ex-Muslim, who goes by the name 'Apostate Prophet' once narrated in a video what happened when he disclosed to his parents in Turkey that he no longer believed in Islam. His parents were strong believers, and he knew they would be shocked, but luckily for him, they didn't kill him. Lucky for him, they didn't follow their book which prescribes death for apostasy. I remember him saying something like 'Fortunately, most Muslims are not as bad as Islam wants them to be.'

It means, the conscience of even strong book-believers has not been fully silenced. What will it take to make more people listen to their inner voice and follow dharma and be well-meaning to ALL?

Chapter 31

The Attacks on Hindus have an Agenda

EVER SINCE I came to know what great wisdom the Hindu tradition contained, I wondered why Hindus so far, have not forcefully objected to being degraded as 'idol-worshippers'. It is an extremely negative term for members of the Abrahamic religions and invites hatred and attacks on Hindus. In 2020, I even drafted a petition to the UN, asking them to declare that it is unacceptable to teach hatred for Hindus in a religious class. I guess, I was naïve. It seems there are powerful, well-organised forces at work which want Hindu Dharma demolished. Why? Probably because it has too much wisdom.

Almost every day, in Pakistan and Bangladesh, Hindus are insulted, attacked, kidnapped, and even killed for being Hindus. World media ignores it. Yet physical attacks also happen in India, where Hindus are the majority.

Temples are desecrated, sadhus are stabbed to death in *mandirs*; Hindu boys, who married Muslim girls, or refused conversion, are mercilessly killed. There was a video clip on the net, where during the CAA protests in January 2020, even

Muslim *women* threatened Hindus, 'The day we Muslims exceed the number of Hindus, we will smash them one by one.' Tarek Fatah tweeted about it at that time with the video clip attached, which meanwhile has been deleted.

Their threat 'to smash Hindus one by one, once Muslims are in the majority', was not an empty threat. It had a precedent in 1989-90 in Kashmir, where Muslims are in the majority. Selective killings of Hindus started and then posters appeared with three options: 'Convert, leave, or get killed'. To show that they meant it, gruesome murders of Hindus were committed. Obviously, they wanted to 'cleanse' the land of kafirs, as mandated by their religion. For example, the Quranic verse 8.39 says, '...fight them till the *Deen* of Allah is established completely'.

Media had obfuscated it. A French journalist, Francois Gautier, who at that time, reported from Kashmir, became a staunch defender of Hindus ever since, because he saw first-hand, how unfair the media was to the Hindus.

At that time, some 400,000 Hindus fled from Kashmir and many of them still live in refugee camps in northern India. It seems that their own country and the world forgot them. Instead, the world hears (and believes) that the Indian Army brutally oppresses the Muslims in Kashmir.

Hardly anyone knows that Kashmir was the land of Rishi Kashyap, where until 800 years ago, the profound philosophy of Kashmir Shaivism had flourished. Hardly anyone knows that there were several waves of expulsion of Hindus during the last 700 years, after a Muslim had usurped the throne. It was not the first time in 1990 that Hindus had to run for their lives, if they wanted to remain Hindus.

The Kashmir Files

But then, something changed. In March 2022, a movie *The Kashmir Files* came out which truthfully depicted what had happened in 1990. Each scene of violence was realistic and based on documents of what had actually happened. The only deviation from reality was that the movie toned down the brutalities. Film director Vivek Agnihotri mentioned for example, that the scene where the killers of a Hindu man force his wife to eat rice soaked with the blood of her husband, was in real life much worse.

However, one thing is for sure: the movie cannot be called propaganda or even 'vulgar propaganda'. Propaganda means that the reality is twisted to influence opinions. For example, it is propaganda when Muslim invaders are portrayed positively. Or when a charismatic film on Jesus, which many missionaries have on their laptops, is shared freely, because it is meant to help with conversions.

However, no person with some common sense can describe the movie, *The Kashmir Files* as propaganda.

However, Nadav Lapid, the head of the jury of the most prestigious Indian Film Festival described it not only as propaganda but as 'vulgar propaganda'. Surely, he knew what 'vulgar propaganda' means. He read out his statement—so that was not off-the-cuff, but obviously planned. And even when Vivek Agnihotri, the director of the movie, challenged him to show any one scene which is not true, he stuck to his comment. Moreover, Nadav Lapid is an Israeli Jew, yet he demeaned the Hindu victims and protected the Muslim perpetrators.

Why?

The reason may be:

The movie was a great success. For the first time, people in India and abroad realised how Kashmiri Hindus had been terrorised and what great injustice was done to them—by Muslims.

Obviously, this makes the usual narrative suspect, which claims that the Muslims of Kashmir are brutally oppressed by the Indian state and deserve the support of the UN and the world.

Have some people, maybe in Pakistan, brainstormed how this Muslim friendly narrative can again gain credibility?

Now imagine: When world media reports that the jury of the most prestigious Indian Film Festival considers *The Kashmir Files* as 'vulgar propaganda', the movie suddenly looks bad. Some Indian journalists, maybe wanting to be politically correct, went along with Lapid, and claimed that the movie quite certainly was 'propaganda'.

People will feel that they were fooled to believe what they were shown. 'Oh, it was only a 'propaganda' film to defame Muslims. How bad of those cunning Hindus,' would be the natural reaction of those who are not well-informed; and the majority of people worldwide are not well-informed.

So naturally, the question is, did Nadav Lapid allow himself to be used or rather, to be bribed? This would explain why he stuck so fiercely to his outrageous, unreasonable comments, even after the Israeli Ambassador told him that he should be ashamed. If Lapid had handlers higher up, surely, they were pleased with him.

Yet there is another dimension, too.

The comment by Lapid is only one of the many attacks on Hindus in recent years. Hindus are accused of being oppressors, divisive, communal, hateful, extremists, fascists, rapists, even terrorists—in short, despicable. Seminars on *Dismantling Global Hindutva* were organised. Arundhati

Roy accused the Modi government in 2020 live on German *Deutsche Welle* of planning genocide of Muslims and asked the world to keep an eye on it. *Quora* had a question, 'Will India become the most hated country?'

On the other hand, Hindus are known to be well-meaning, kind, helpful, intelligent, and business-savvy. They are seen as the ideal immigrants who easily adapt and contribute much to their host countries. And in India, they kept a genuine democracy going against all doomsday prophecies, and lifted the country out of abject poverty, which the British Raj had left as its legacy.

So why are these attacks happening?

The reason may be that India is the last surviving ancient culture and has still a lot of valuable knowledge. All other ancient cultures—Incas, Mayas, Aztecs, Greeks, Egyptians, Mesopotamians, or Chinese, have been destroyed in a relatively short time either by Christianity, Islam, or Communism.

Yet in India, the fight is still going on since centuries. Big parts of Greater India have fallen, and life there is very painful for the remaining Hindus. As I was writing this, even as recently as December 2024, Hindus in Bangladesh were being lynched, women raped, temples and businesses destroyed, and the caretaker government of Mohammed Yunus was turning a blind eye to all these atrocities. It even claimed that the reports were exaggerated, and basically, conveyed that India should mind its own business. Typically, the world media was silent.

Why is there so much effort to get rid of the Hindu tradition? Shouldn't people be happy that at least one ancient culture has survived, a culture which has preserved valuable texts and has a profound philosophy?

Unfortunately, the powerful Left, the Church, and Islam,

all wish to wipe out Hinduism, which is portrayed as bad even without them understanding its profound philosophy.

Or, do they understand its profound philosophy and consider it an impediment to their agenda?

For example, the Pope may not believe what he tells his flock about the Christian doctrine. Surely, he knows that Hinduism is not bad, but rather too good. He knows that it empowers and if people came to know the truth about it, they would choose it over Christianity.

In all likelihood, the Pope and the others on top of the pyramid, who are used to controlling people, don't want strong, intuitive, joyful humans, who think for themselves.

Leftist media and Western education have almost succeeded in making 'Hindu' sound like a dirty word, and many educated Indians feel apologetic for being Hindus.

Yet some 15 years ago, thanks to the internet, Hindus realised that Hinduism, which was always portrayed as less worthy than the Abrahamic religions, is the better option for humanity. Many Hindus became vocal and proud about it. Ever since, attempts to portray Hindus in a bad light, and outright attacks have intensified. The war for supremacy is still on.

What can Hindus do against opponents of Hinduism, who have a military-style strategy to achieve their goal of dismantling the most benign faith and culture? Hindus tend to rely on *Satyameva Jayate*—truth will triumph. This is true, but it doesn't mean that we should sit idle, and not help the truth from coming to light.

It's time to be clear and truthful, and we must not be afraid to call out the basic faults of the Abrahamic religions in a proactive manner, faults which I have already detailed earlier and won't repeat here. Only this much: Islam and

Christianity demean all Hindus as kafirs and idol-worshippers and predict a terrible fate for them in future, which is ordained by the creator of the universe himself. Such attitude makes genocide possible.

We must also not be afraid to call out the nefarious plans of the Deep State, where Jews like Klaus Schwab or George Soros are prominent. Others are in the background, like the Rothschild family, which has gained immeasurable wealth by looting Bharat through the East India Company.

George Soros openly said at the World Economic Forum in Davos, that the nationalist Hindu government in India is bad news. This surely means that great efforts will be made—and money is absolutely no constraint for them—to get India in line with the planned international communist New World Order, where Hindu Dharma will have no place.

Can Hindus drive the narrative, instead of being driven?

Can we demand that Christianity and Islam drop the untrue, divisive dogmas and that these dogmas not be taught to children?

Can we, including well-known gurus, support courageous people like Waseem Rizvi, who went to court claiming that many verses in the Quran are hateful? Or, do we still have doubts whether these verses are indeed hateful? If so, please get a copy in a language you understand.

Or, do we feel, 'Let Muslims and Christians sort it out among themselves'? This probably is cowardice and not some virtue.

Can the Hindu panellists call a spade a spade in TV debates, and can we also, in talks with friends of different communities, have the courage to talk freely about religious topics? No doubt, we still need to be circumspect, because we may end up in hiding, like Nupur Sharma, a former BJP spokeswoman, who mentioned in a TV debate the well-known fact of Mohammed's relation with his 9-year-old wife, Aisha. Or even worse, end up like the tailor Kanhaiyalal Teli and the chemist Umesh Kolbe with their throats slit for supporting Nupur Sharma on social media.

Sadly, Muslims and Christians in Bharat do not realise that they are only pawns in a bigger game to destroy the ancient Hindu tradition. It is in their own interest when the dharma of their ancestors not only survives, but flourishes. The focus needs to be on devotion for and trust in the Supreme Being and not on the different names for it. And who knows, maybe someday, they will realise the value of their ancestors' wisdom and will be glad, that their Hindu brothers and sisters have preserved it.

Chapter 32

Divisive Forces and Hateful Voices

IITs (INDIAN INSTITUTE OF TECHNOLOGY) and IIMs (Indian Institute of Management) are the topmost educational institutions in India. The entrance test is exceptionally tough, especially for the IITs. A German math professor once showed on video, questions for the IIT entrance test and claimed that even German math teachers would not pass. But not only the IITs, the IIMs also have an excellent reputation. The alumni and of course the professors in these institutions belong to the intellectual elite not only in India, but worldwide.

So, I was genuinely happy when I read that faculty and students of IIMs had written a letter to PM Modi, asking him to speak up against divisive forces and hateful voices. Though I was aware that politicians and media inexplicably often blame Hindus as being divisive, I was sure that members of these premier institutions would see through what is happening and get it right.

My hope was dashed. They had also got it wrong.

An article in the *Indian Express*, on 8 January 2022 caught my eye. It was titled *Your silence emboldens hate voices: Faculty, students of IIMs to PM*[8].

Sixteen Professors and 167 students of IIM Ahmedabad and Bangalore had signed a letter and sent it to the Prime Minister's Office. It urged PM Modi to steer the country away from 'forces that seek to divide us', and rued, 'Your silence, Honourable Prime Minister, emboldens the hate-filled voices and threatens the unity and integrity of our country.'

Two years earlier, I had also written a letter to the Prime Minister and had attached a draft for a petition to the United Nations with a similar request. I had focused on the contempt and the resultant hatred for Hindus which is inbuilt in the doctrines of Christianity and Islam. I know it firsthand since I grew up as a Christian. Hindus are seen as nonbelievers, even though most Hindus are great believers in the Divine, because for those religions, 'nonbelievers' means those who do not believe in Christianity or Islam, respectively.

Both these religions are divisive because they divide humanity into those who are right and saved by the Almighty, and those who are wrong and will be punished by the Almighty.

Both religions claim that Hindus belong to the second category. For them, Hindus are despicable, sinful idol-worshippers who will suffer in hell for all eternity.

---

8   https://indianexpress.com/article/india/silence-hate-voices-iims-to-pm-7712317/

I had argued in my draft that teaching children these divisive claims would create hatred and lead to hate crimes if not genocide. This is not far-fetched. Genocide was committed in India by Muslim and Christian invaders for about 1,000 years, when millions of Hindus were brutally tortured and killed for being Hindus.

The petition draft, which is on my blog (mariawirth.com), contains the following paragraph:

'The unrelenting, unjust vilification of Hindus and Hindutva (Hindu-ness) by the leftist media in support of these two religions puts Hindus in a dangerous position. Hate speech against a group precedes hate crimes and genocide. It needs to be stopped urgently.' So, when I saw this article in the *Indian Express*, I was happy that professors and students of the prestigious IIMs had finally taken up the cause of the unacceptable contempt and hatred for Hindus, since there is no doubt that the two exclusive religions, each of which claims that it alone is true, are divisive forces.

However, while reading the article, I soon realised that these professors and students seemed to live in another world. A world which is upside down, where the victims are the perpetrators and the perpetrators are the victims.

In short, the professors, who drafted the letter, believe that Hindus are hate-filled and attack Muslims and Christians. They point to speeches by sadhus, and some lynching of Muslims by Hindus. Yes, these happen occasionally. For example, when Muslims steal cows and villagers go after them. But more often, it happens that Hindus are lynched, not for stealing or committing crimes, but simply for being Hindus or for resisting conversion.

The speech by sadhus at the *Dharam Sansad* in Haridwar,

to which the signatories of the letter objected, can be seen as an alarmed reaction to equally or more terrible speeches which were made by Muslims and Christians in plenty and which openly expressed their intent to wipe out Hindus, but which strangely are not flagged by these professors and students as hateful.

Why is this bias prevalent in the educated class in India?

Don't those signatories remember, for example the Muslim women at the CAA protest in Delhi, saying on video that when they will be a majority, they will kill Hindus one by one? Or, Waris Pathan, the spokesman for Owaisi, who openly challenged Hindus that if the 15 crore Muslims take to the streets, they would be enough to bring down the 100 crores of the country to their knees? (He didn't mention 'Hindus', but the intent was clear). Don't those professors and students know that it is the duty of good Muslims to wage jihad and leave only Muslims on earth and that it is also the duty of good Christians to wipe out beliefs in 'false gods'?

There are umpteen hate-filled speeches against Hindus on the net, not only by Muslims but also by Christians. For example, a priest of the Pentecostal Church in Tamil Nadu asked all the members to convert Hindus, so that in three years, the whole of Tamil Nadu is converted. In the *Blessings Magazine* (March 2009 issue) of the Baptist Church, the youth was exhorted that 'India must be converted in this generation'.

Have the signatories forgotten the lynching of the sadhus and their driver in Palghar right in front of policemen? Or, the many *pujaris* who were murdered and their temples desecrated? The many rapes and murders of Hindu girls? Or, Ramalingam, a youth from Tamil Nadu, who was murdered since he had objected to conversion and many others like him from the RSS?

Do those signatories not know about the history of the last thousand years?

I can't even attempt to detail the cruelties by Muslims and Christians, as it would need the length of an entire book to do so. Even in the last hundred years, the list is terrible—the brutal Hindu genocide by Moplahs in 1921, the 'Direct Action Day' in 1946 in Kolkata, the partition in 1947…the unspeakable brutalities against Hindus in Bangladesh in 1971, and now again, in 2024, after the coup against the Sheikh Hasina government. The genocide in Kashmir in 1990, which resulted in 4 lakh Kashmiri Hindus fleeing their homes. The huge provocation in April 2025 in Pahalgam, where 26 unsuspecting Hindu men on vacation with their families, were shot dead, point blank…

Apart from these mass persecution and killing of Hindus, individual Hindus keep being killed. A few weeks ago, someone posted on X the names of 60 Hindus who were killed in recent months by Muslims only for being Hindu—in Bharat, where they are the majority.

Dear students and professors of IIMs, please introspect.
Compare the above facts with what Hindus did to Muslims and Christians and have some integrity and honesty. Think of your ancestors who suffered greatly for holding on to their dharma, and who may have had to open their mouths and humbly receive the spittle of Muslims who passed them on horseback (I read this and other barbaric methods to humiliate Hindus in *Legacy of Jihad* by Andrew G Bostom).

Thanks to your ancestors, Hindu civilisation is still alive, though it has shrunk significantly, especially due to many violent Muslim invasions. A huge number of Muslims in today's world had Hindu ancestors. In 2023, there were about 360 million Arab Muslims. Pakistan and India together have already many more. Then add to them the Muslims of Bangladesh, Afghanistan, Indonesia, Malaysia…

It's really sad that you support those who attack Hindu Dharma and thereby risk to make Indian Hindus and possibly yourself suffer in a few decades in similar depraved circumstances, as the unfortunate few remaining Hindus in Pakistan or Bangladesh do. Afghanistan can pride itself that it has already fulfilled its religious duty and has wiped out Hindus from its soil.

Your letter says 'Our Constitution gives us the right to practice our religion with dignity—without fear, without shame. There is a sense of fear in our country now—places of worship, including Churches in recent days, are being vandalised, and there have been calls to take arms against our Muslim brothers and sisters. All of this is carried out with impunity and without any fear of the due process.'

Please introspect who is victimising whom. Surely, you consider yourself highly educated, but there are gaps in your education. Read about the history and about the fundamentals of Hindu Dharma and the fundamentals of those religions which claim that they alone are true and all must follow them. Also, read and listen to media with the required discernment.

Then you may come to a more realistic understanding.

Chapter 33

A Strange Question on Quora
Is India becoming the most hated country?

AFTER THE Nirbhaya rape and murder in 2012, a massive campaign was launched to stigmatise Indians, and specifically Hindus, as rapists. The impact of this campaign was extraordinarily 'successful'. In March 2015, a biochemistry professor at the University of Leipzig in Germany refused admission to an Indian student to her course because of India's 'rape problem'. It turned out that this was not the only case.

The 'Indians are rapists' campaign started soon after the news about the Rotherham 'sex grooming gangs' of mainly Pakistani Muslim men had come out in the open. I wondered if the person, who asked this dubious question on Quora, wanted to know how well the business of maligning India had progressed, and if India is on the way to becoming the most hated country.

My reply to the question 'Is India becoming the most hated country?' got 40,000 views within 24 hours, which was exceptionally high. Yet, from one moment to another, the views suddenly stagnated. I got a message from a person with a Muslim name, asking me to drop the last sentence of my post.

I didn't do it, because what I had written was the truth. Next, I got a message that my reply was removed by Quora. Later, Quora also removed the question. Maybe Hindus had successfully objected to such a biased, hateful question.

Here is my reply:

Oh no, India can never become the most hated country—never mind how much media, missionaries, and other vested interests try to portray it as such.

There are too many people in the world who have been to India, who know her profound philosophy, who know how much she has contributed to civilisation (more than any other country in this world), who know how kind and open-minded her people are, how they live and let live which includes millions of cows, monkeys, stray dogs, even tigers, leopards, elephants, snakes, etc… in spite of a huge population on little space.

Too many people know how colourful and joyful the atmosphere is during the many festivals, which mostly have a religious nature, they know how alive the country is, and how generously India shares her knowledge like Yoga or Ayurveda, how amazing her culture is—music, dance, sculpture, architecture and more. Also, there are too many people who know Indians who live abroad and know that they are among the best immigrants possible.

But yes, attempts are on to portray India in a very poor light. 'Rapes in India' and 'atrocities against minorities' are preferred news on foreign TV channels, for example on Deutsche Welle or BBC, when the same channels won't broadcast the rapes that happen in their own countries.

Recently, a poll in England showed that Indians are seen positively (+2, 5), while Pakistanis are seen negatively (-4).

The amazing thing is that Indians and Pakistanis are basically the same people. The only difference is that some Indians converted to Islam during the Muslim rule of their country. At the time of Independence, those who had converted to Islam demanded their own country as they did not want to live with the Hindus. And, while hardly any Hindus are left in Pakistan, India allowed Muslims, who did not want to move to Pakistan, to stay on, and ever since their numbers have been increasing significantly.

So, maybe there is one condition: **India can never become the most hated country as long as Hindus remain the majority.**

I had been asked to remove this last sentence.

As an afterthought: Indians and Pakistanis have 'the same DNA', but Hindu children hear from childhood that they need to follow dharma, which means to do what feels right according to their conscience. In contrast, Muslim children hear from childhood that they must follow what their holy book says—and it says repeatedly, that 'non-Muslims' are despicable and Allah doesn't like them being on earth and will punish them greatly.

It's the mindset which makes the difference.

Chapter 34

No Place for Truth in Political Correctness

MANY YEARS ago, I had my horoscope made. It said among other things that I am courageous. I thought, it referred to my many travels to far away countries all alone. As an intern with Lufthansa, I paid only 10 per cent of the ticket fare, and some airlines gave tickets even for free, so naturally, I used this chance to see the world to the utmost. Yet, though others often called it courageous, it did not feel courageous to me.

Meanwhile, I realised that there is something that indeed requires courage: to speak what one considers the truth. It was not like this some decades ago. 'Political correctness' was not an issue during the 1970s when I studied at university and we had heated debates over pizza or coffee. Yet over time, political correctness sneaked into the discourse, so much so, that now, especially people in the West, are frightened to say what they think. Luckily, the situation is better in Bharat.

Some years ago, on a visit to Germany, I met with a few friends from my primary school times. Two of them I hadn't seen for over 50 years, but we were quickly familiar again, after we got used to our new (elderly) look.

The conversation turned to the Turks in town, around 600 of the overall 6,000 inhabitants. 'Most of the Turks are not integrating into our society, and they get help from Turkey to buy houses right in the centre of the town. Recently, they bought the pub German Empire, which is now their community centre—a kind of a symbolic triumph over Germany,' a former classmate said.

I replied that ever since I read the Quran, I have become wary of pious Muslims. Those who believe what is written there, will never see non-Muslims as equals. They are simply not allowed to. They will have to strive to gain majority wherever they live and then bully the others into submission, if we are lucky not to be killed first.

There was silence for a while. Then a former classmate said: 'Maria, I think exactly like you. But I wouldn't have dared to say what you just said.'

Her comment brought home the power of mass media.

For decades, all over the world, 'political correctness' has been drummed into us, but especially in the West, where many have internalised what they are allowed to say and what not. Maybe, we did not even notice that we have voluntarily surrendered the right to free speech, which is one of the greatest plus points of modern societies.

Who can be freely attacked and who not, is one of the incomprehensible features of political correctness. In spite of the fact that Hindus were victims for centuries under the Muslim and British rule with millions of them being killed; in spite of the fact that Hindus never went on the offensive in the name of their Gods, they and their tradition are today fair game for verbal attacks which are clearly hate speeches but are hardly ever persecuted as such.

In contrast, antisemitism is absolutely not tolerated. In May 2024, the US Senate even passed a Bill to outlaw any criticism not only of Jews but even of Israel in the face of protests against the war on Gaza.

Holocaust denial is a crime in several countries. Germany is extra strict: One gets jailed even if one asks questions about the Holocaust. It happened to Ursula Haverbeck. She had asked for evidence of the gas chambers from German and Jewish institutions for several years, and when she didn't get any replies, she publicly expressed her doubt regarding the official narrative, in a video. She was arrested and jailed for two years, in spite of being over 90 years of age. Since she did not change her view, in June 2024, she was again sentenced to another 16 months, but she passed away before starting her second jail term. According to her, there are around two thousand people in German prisons for doubting the holocaust narrative.

Yet, apart from Jews, inexplicably, Muslims and Islam are also protected against negative comments. This surprises all the more since mainstream media is largely in Jewish hands, whom Muslims want to 'drive into the sea'. Why then do they give this velvet-glove treatment to Muslims, and even project Islam as a religion of peace?

In a balanced debate it would become clear that Hindu Dharma is far better placed as a religion of peace. Yet, did you ever hear that 'Hinduism is a religion of peace'? And if you say it, not only non-Hindus, but also politically correct Hindus immediately remind you of the 'atrocious caste system'.

How did we reach a state where we can no longer have a meaningful debate on what is true and reasonable? Has truth been thrown out of the window? It seems like that.

Indeed, now the 'correct' line is that 'There is no truth as such. Rather, there are many truths.' It's called moral or ethical relativism. Whatever somebody claims, is his or her truth and needs to be respected. If you have a male body but you claim you are a woman, you need to be treated as a woman.

When I mentioned to a German friend from my study times that nowadays it needs courage to speak the truth, I was taken aback when he replied, 'There is no truth as such'. I tried to make him see that though the Absolute Truth (attributeless Brahman) cannot be put into words, yet on the relative maya level, a lie is not the truth, even if somebody believes in it. Steadfastly ignoring important facts to create a different perception of an issue is also dishonest and akin to a lie.

'*Satyam vada, Dharam chara*' is an ancient advice from the *Taittiriya Upanishad*—speak the truth and do what is right.

Is it so difficult to find out whether the politically correct view is truthful or not?

For example, let's take the concern to empower women. It's a worthy concern. But what happened in the name of feminism and gender equality, clearly went overboard and has become harmful. Unequal laws were enacted which favour women and put men in danger of landing innocently in jail because their side of the story simply does not count.

My taxi driver told me an experience he had:

A woman waved him down at a bus stop in Delhi, when he was going back empty to Dehradun after dropping a passenger at the airport. He stopped, and she quickly got in and told him to continue on the road. He started driving and asked her where she wanted to go. She again said, 'continue straight'.

He told her, 'Tell me the address or I will drop you off now.'

Her reply, 'I will get down, but only after you give me Rs 300.'

He was shocked and said that he will call the police.

'Okay, call the police. I will tell them what you did to me,' she said.

He knew he was trapped. The police would listen to her and not to him. He gave her Rs 300, and she left.

He considered himself fortunate that he got away with just paying Rs 300. Other men had found themselves in far worse traps. Sadly, many even committed suicide.

The story of Atul Subhash was especially heartbreaking. It made big waves in media and on the internet, because he had planned everything systematically. He had minutely recorded an 80-minute video which showed the injustice and harassment that was meted out to him by his wife and even by the judge. He also wrote it down in 24-pages with proofs, and put it all on the net, before he ended his life. He saw no other way to be heard.

As a consequence of laws favouring women, and at the same time, pushing toxic feminism, the trust between men and women has suffered, and in Western societies, the family system has almost gone bust. There, many people feel lonely and lost. Yet any criticism of feminism is shouted down.

Meanwhile, in Western countries, not only feminism, but also LGTBQ+ and even sex changes in children get protection by the media, academia, and the medical fraternity. However, right after assuming office in January 2025, Trump has taken steps to curb this 'woke culture' in the USA.

Unfortunately, the fear of being politically incorrect makes people go along with so-called 'progressive views', even when they are not comfortable with them. It seems there is an attempt to bully people into accepting a defunct, conformist, and ultimately debased society, where even the sexualisation of children is the norm.

Recently, I talked with an old school friend about the highly immoral 1920s in Berlin. What happened in Berlin one hundred years ago, was a precursor to the moral and sexual depravity that is happening now in the West and which is also being pushed into Bharat.

After losing the first World War and with inflation being sky-high, most Germans were extremely poor. Prostitution was a means to survive, as all types of foreigners streamed into Berlin to buy whatever depravity they could think of for just a few dollars. An institute for sexual research came up and postulated already then, in the 1920s, many different genders (the books of the institute were later burnt by the Nazis).

At first, my friend tried to see it in a positive light. She said, 'well, it had the advantage that finally gays were openly accepted'. I replied that certain things should not be aired in public, and there is no need to shout about being gay or anything else. She immediately agreed, and also felt that things have gone too far and this focus on sexuality is not healthy for any society.

So, let's not be swayed by political correctness and let's have the courage to speak the truth.

Satyameva Jayate!

Chapter 35

Rebirth is for Real–Within Maya

THERE ARE three major differences between Hindu Dharma and the Abrahamic religions. The most important is:
'God' is within you as pure, blissful Consciousness.
The second major difference is the belief in rebirth.
And the third is the stress laid on sattvic, pure food as it influences the mind. Vegetarian food is clearly recommended.

The first point has been explained in the earlier chapters. In the following chapter, good reasons are given why rebirth is for real—within Maya.

I don't remember which Bollywood movie it was. There were two heroes wooing one heroine, and naturally one hero had to die in the end because she could not marry both. As it happened, one indeed died. It was a sad ending. He was a nice guy. But before the credits started rolling on the screen, a voice boomed through the movie hall, *'Vapis aega—dusre roop mein.'* (He will come back in another form). It brought in a philosophical angle. The movie had not touched me, yet this last sentence gave me goosebumps.

Right from the beginning of my stay in India, I felt that here death is not so terrifying. Of course, there is fear of death, and Indians suffer when a dear family member or friend is lost. Yet death is not as final, as in the West, because of the belief that those who have died will be reborn. This is not blind belief. There are many good arguments in favour of it.

For example, the Law of Karma, makes much more sense when it is not applied to only one life. The differences between human beings appear in a different light. Why is someone born in a palace and another in a hut? Why does one baby have loving parents and another does not? Why is one person bright, and another, retarded? Such questions lead many people to despair about a just God. Yet, rebirth gives a reasonable explanation. Everything is in a flux. Who cries today, may laugh tomorrow, and who laughs today, may cry tomorrow.

A vast body of research exists on the subject. Some 3,000 cases of rebirth have been studied and filed in the archives of the Division of Perceptual Studies of the University of Virginia, USA. Ian Stevenson, who passed away in 2007, was the initiator and main authority of the studies. He worked with researchers around the globe.

Their research came to the conclusion that rebirth is the most plausible and most rational interpretation of their findings. This conclusion was nothing new for Indians, yet in the West, this theory received a mixed response. Many Western scientists still refuse to consider the possibility of rebirth due to their brainwashing in childhood that there is only one life.

Ian Stevenson's greatest frustration was not that people dismissed his theories, but that most did so without even reading the evidence which he had gathered. 'Either Stevenson is making a colossal mistake, or he will be known...as 'the Galileo of the twentieth century,' a psychiatrist wrote. It shows that academics in the West are either like frogs in a well or extremely arrogant. A great part of humanity takes rebirth for granted. Yet this academician feels that Stevenson will be credited with discovering it if this theory is ever confirmed.

In India, Professor N K Chadha of Delhi University worked with Ian Stevenson. I met him in 1989 and he explained how he proceeds with his research:

Occasionally, it happens that a child of only 3 or 4 years, claims with absolute conviction that he is a certain grown-up person whose name is such and such and who lived and died in such and such way. Once the professor's team gets to know about it, they visit the child, gather information, and try to identify the person described; and if identified, crosscheck all the inside information. It is a lot of work. Countless visits may have to be made to a far-flung village to rule out any other explanations of why this child has amazing inside knowledge about a person who had died before his birth.

A case is considered solved, when the person, who the child claims to have been, is identified, all inside knowledge crosschecked and no discrepancies are found. Then it can be safely assumed that the child 'remembers' what he knows about that person, and it is considered a case of rebirth.

Prof Chadha had examined twenty-five cases out of which eleven had been 'solved' at that time. Those cases are fascinating. I am outlining here the case of Titu Singh:

Titu was born in December 1983 in a village near Agra. As soon as he could speak, he started claiming that his name was Suresh Verma, and that he owned a radio shop in Agra, and that one evening, when he came home, he was shot dead.

Further, he said, he has two sons and a wife named Uma. He spoke in detail about how he died. He said, he had driven home in his Fiat and honked so that his wife would open the gate. Suddenly, two men came running and fired at him. One bullet hit him in his head.

Titu was aggressive towards his 'new' parents. He did not accept them as his parents. He stubbornly maintained that his 'real' parents lived in Agra. Finally, Titu's elder brother went to Agra and was shocked to find, that indeed, there was a 'Suresh Radio Shop' in the bazaar. He gathered information: the owner, a certain Suresh Verma had died in August 1983, exactly the way that Titu had described. Uma, Suresh's widow, was curious to see the boy who claimed to be her husband, reborn. She went with her parents-in-law and Suresh's three brothers to Titu's village.

Titu immediately ran towards 'his parents' and embraced them. He shyly glanced at Uma and then disappointed, he turned to his brothers. 'Why did you come in this car and not in my Fiat?' he asked petulantly. The family had sold the Fiat after Suresh's death.

Titu was taken to Agra. The brothers, all adults, intended to drive past the radio shop to test him. However, the four-year-old pounced on the driver, 'Stop! Here is my shop', he shouted. Inside, he commented on some changes that had been made after Suresh's death.

Prof Chadha and Dr Antonia Mills of Virginia University examined the case over almost four years to rule out that Titu had got his information through normal communication. They watched him and his reactions closely.

Once, when Prof Chadha asked little Titu to greet Mahesh, Suresh's thirty-five-year-old younger brother, he refused. 'He is my younger brother' the child protested. The researchers came to know that the relationship between Mahesh and Suresh had been tense. This explained why Titu usually ignored Mahesh.

Significantly, Mahesh was the only member of the Verma family who had some doubts. Mahesh speculated that since Suresh was known in Agra, everyone knew about the murder, so Titu's parents could have fed this information to their son, maybe to get some financial benefits from the Vermas who were wealthier than the Singhs. But he could not hold on to this theory for long.

He changed his stand after he tested Titu. He grabbed Titu's wrist, Prof Chadha narrated, and did not let go of it. 'Tell me, what happened during my wedding?' he demanded to know. The boy reacted annoyed. 'Why, nothing happened. I threw plates.' Now, Mahesh was also convinced. It was true. Suresh had spoiled the atmosphere of the wedding when he had angrily thrown plates around.

The research into rebirth discovered that in about four out of ten rebirth cases, the child remembered a sudden death, either through an accident or murder which happened at an average age of 34 years. The interval between death and rebirth was also significantly shorter than if the person had died peacefully.

If one is unexpectedly pulled out from one's body, there may be the feeling that one has not yet finished with living their current life and wants to return as soon as possible to 'continue' living. The great interest in the previous life and the short span between death and birth may make the memory easier to access and therefore the identification with the earlier person overshadows his present life.

'Do you personally believe in rebirth?' I asked Prof Chadha.

'Yes', he said without hesitation. Most Indians do not need 'scientific' proof. Rebirth is clearly the best explanation for all the differences between humans.

Yet, in spite of all the evidence for rebirth, there is no rebirth on another, higher level of truth. 'Find out, whether you have been born in this life,' the sage Ramana Maharshi exhorted a visitor who wanted to know about his previous births. And when once asked, whether there is rebirth, Ramana had replied, 'There is rebirth and there is no rebirth.'

He probably meant that on the appearance (or maya) level, rebirth is a fact. In terms of Absolute Truth, where there is only One Infinite Conscious Being, there is no place for different persons to be born and reborn.

Chapter 36

Amnesia of Animal Eaters

DOES ANYONE remember the photo of several Youth Congress members walking down a street in Kerala with a calf in their midst? It was reported that they had cut the throat of the calf right there in public. Sometimes one wonders where Bharat is headed. Those youths probably considered themselves 'progressive'.

I have to admit that I had been eating meat before I came to Bharat. I didn't know any better. It seemed normal, right from childhood. Only in Bharat, I realised how thoughtless I had been about the suffering of the slaughtered animals and how indoctrinated in believing that meat protein is needed for health. And, how hypocritical we generally are in our 'love' for animals.

I wrote this article some 15 years ago and did not update the numbers, as the exact numbers are not important. I can't help feeling that our lack of compassion and outright cruelty towards animals will haunt us humans and make us suffer.

Some time ago, a man in the US was sentenced to six months in jail for tying his dog to his car and dragging him to death. The dog had 'barked too much' which made his owner furious. Neighbours chased the man. They were rightly upset by his cruel act and, except for some perverse and pathological misfits, every human will surely condemn such brutal treatment of animals.

However, this news item reminded me of a German saying: 'What I don't see does not agitate me.' In all likelihood, the neighbours of that American were eating meat. Are meat eaters aware of the heartbreaking life and finally the brutal slaughter of all those chickens, cows, pigs, sheep, or goats in the so-called meat industry?

Probably they vaguely are, yet somehow it does not get at them. It seems one needs to be personally involved with one chicken or one cow, see the suffering, look into her anguished eyes, to realise the cruelty and then resolve not to partake in it anymore.

It happened to a young German couple who had been on a camel safari in Rajasthan. The father of the girl had been my colleague during my internship at Lufthansa, so the couple visited me and told me about the safari.

Their narration centred only on one thing: the chicken. 'Do you want chicken for dinner?' the agent had asked. 'Okay', they had answered, not guessing what this would entail.

They started on their camel ride with great anticipation. Soon they noticed that a chicken was tied to one camel, legs up, head down. The chicken was clearly miserable and as the day progressed, it lost its feathers, turned bluish, and was half dead but still alive.

My young friends could think of nothing else but the chicken. They felt so sorry for it. Their safari was spoilt. In the evening, the chicken was cooked but they could not eat it. 'I don't think I can ever eat a chicken again,' the woman said.

In India, animals are out in the open, in contrast to the so-called developed West where most people even in small towns see only pet dogs or cats and never come face to face with a cow or even a hen in their whole life. In India, everyone comes close to cows, goats, pigs, monkeys, dogs, hens, camels and elephants—and foreign tourists sometimes get very incensed at their treatment.

They feel pity for the stray dogs, condemn the neglect of the cows that wander the streets, and are furious at the animal sacrifices which are still practised in a few temples in Eastern India. I agree, it is terrible to see low cages by the roadside, crammed with hens that can't move, or a goat tied in front of a butcher's shop where it will be killed soon after, or a truck being intercepted that is packed tight with smuggled cows intended for slaughter.

Yet, India is still the one country standing out in the world: it has the greatest percentage of vegetarians and is, therefore, comparatively good to animals. By far the greater (legal) crime of even unimaginable proportions is committed in the Western world, and Christianity is a partner in this crime by declaring that creation is meant to serve man.

Islam and Judaism also consider the killing of animals for food, normal, and they do it in an extra painful way to make the flesh *halal* or *kosher*. On the festival of Bakr Eid, the throat of an animal is cut within the homes in the presence of children 'in a festive spirit of sacrifice', as news anchors smilingly proclaim. Does that refer to the sacrificing of one's innate compassion towards living beings and becoming insensitive to their suffering?

However, in the West, the killing of animals is hidden and euphemised in language. It is a clever business strategy, because who would like to know that he chews on a corpse of an animal that had a pitiful life? So, the meat is neatly packaged and sold off from giant supermarket freezers where one never thinks that it was ever connected to a former living being. Nobody, except those who work in the 'meat industry', is confronted with the brutality involved in the killing of animals for meat. Those who eat meat, and in the West, most do, betray total amnesia about the torture and slaughter of 'livestock'.

Swami Chidanand Saraswati of Parmarth Niketan Ashram in Rishikesh wrote a small book titled *Vegetarianism: For your body, your mind, your soul, and your planet*, which gives us some chilling facts. In USA alone, some 20 million chickens and 90,000 cows are butchered every day. In a year over 10 billion animals are slaughtered in USA alone. The numbers are inconceivable and don't convey the suffering and fear of any one of those creatures who have done no harm to us.

We might condone the killings with the argument that in nature, too, one species feeds on another. Yet the human species is certainly the worst. In a majority of the cases, we don't need the meat. In fact, we would be healthier without it. We eat it for pleasure and don't even think about what it entails. Swami Chidanand mentions that the national news network in the US broadcast videotapes of the world's biggest meat packing company.

'The tapes showed struggling, conscious cows being hoisted upside down and their throat slit… fully conscious cows were skinned alive, their legs cut off while struggling for freedom. Cows were shown being hit repeatedly with stunning devices that did not work. Other cows were tortured and repeatedly shocked with cattle prods and workers were shown shoving an electric prod into a cow's mouth.'

There would be much more to quote from his book about the miserable lives and the terrible treatment meted out to calves, pigs, geese, turkeys, and hens by the big agriculture industry. It churns one's stomach to just read about it, and thanks to books like the one by Swami Chidanand or Twitter posts with photos, people have become more aware. Finally, vegetarianism is on the rise in the West.

Unfortunately, in India, the opposite is true and meat eaters are on the rise. According to a study by *Newsweek*, the number of chicken eaters in India had doubled between 2000 and 2007. Maybe eating chicken or a hamburger is considered cool and modern, like drinking cola or eating chips. In India, it is known, unlike in the West, that what one eats influences the mind, yet more and more people ignore this fact or have already forgotten it. The results of eating junk food on one's physical and mental health are meanwhile (in 2025) visible. Obesity has skyrocketed in Bharat.

Just think of the sad life and fear the animal experiences before it is killed. Do you really want to eat it? Besides, digesting meat takes up to 72 hours. Just imagine it rotting in your body for three days at a temperature of 37 degrees Celsius.

A study found that vegetarians have a better body odour than meat eaters. Of course, this makes sense, and it didn't need a study for this.

It is acknowledged that a vegetarian diet is healthier for the body and the mind. It also helps in feeding many more people, as across the world, an average 40 per cent of the grain that is harvested is used to 'produce' meat.

And, it is better for one's spirit if one does not indirectly support that colossal bloodbath that is happening day in and day out. Probably, most people would stop eating meat if they saw what had happened to the animal that ends up on their plate.

Campaigning for animal rights is incomplete and insincere when it includes only those animals that are out in the open and excludes those animal brothers and sisters that are hidden away in huge farms, silently suffering before being brutally butchered and eaten by animal eaters in a 'civilised' manner with a fork and knife on white, starched table cloths.

Hindus need to know that there are forces who want to wean them away from spirituality. Becoming insensitive to the suffering of animals by eating their flesh is a step in this direction.

Recently, alert Indian parents discovered that in a picture book for toddlers in kindergarten, a cow was described as: 'She eats grass. We drink her milk and can eat her flesh.'

The school apologised and removed the book from the curriculum.

Chapter 37

India's Holy Cows

IT KEEPS happening that some Indians with Hindu names try to trigger traditional Hindus by posting pictures of themselves eating beef. Eating the flesh of a cow is an absolute 'No-No' for any self-respecting Hindu. Twitter (now X) seems to boost such tweets, which are painful for Hindus.

Moreover, dubious research is quoted that ancient Indians used to eat beef.

This question was asked on Quora:

Is eating beef right, as some Vedas allow Hindus to do so?

Quora removed my reply as being against their policy of being nice and respectful. Please see if there is anything not nice or not respectful in my reply:

Eating beef is not right, and I wonder where are those 'some Vedas' which allow Hindus to do so. Please keep in mind that there were and still are vested interests who want to weaken Hindus and who use wrong translations and interpolations of the ancient texts to make Hindus ashamed of their traditions. Many educated Hindus believe those translations.

I grew up in the West and there we were indoctrinated by Christian tenets (and Muslims and Jews by their religious tenets) that nature, including animals, is there to serve man who is considered 'the crown of creation'. The result is a brutal bloodbath all over the world with billions of animals being slaughtered daily. Each single one of them dies a painful death. It is considered normal.

Do we have the moral right to do this?

Hindu Dharma requires one to use intelligence. It is not a fixed belief system. It doesn't have commandments, which need to be followed or else one lands eternally in hellfire. But yes, Hindu Dharma has rules that are to be followed if you want to make your life into an ideal life.

The law of karma makes sense. Even Christianity copied 'As you sow, so shall you reap'. Anandmayi Ma used to say that the reaction to an action will find the doer of the action, as 'a calf finds its mother among thousand cows'.

So, the choice is ours. Hinduism doesn't threaten with eternal hell if we eat meat, but it will be in our own interest (and in the interest of the animals and the world's ecology) if we stick to vegetarianism unless we need meat for survival.

The Indian rishis realised that a cow is special—like a mother, gentle, and giving and with the most beautiful, kind eyes. Everything the cow gives is useful and has medicinal benefits, including its urine and dung. Her nature is sattvic or pure. Who would kill her? Who would kill any animal unless necessary for some compelling reasons?

Humanity would be more human if this massive brutal slaughter was at least reduced if not fully stopped.

In a video by Agniveer, it is beautifully explained, while interspersed with the chanting of relevant *shlokas*, what the

Vedas say about animal slaughter and eating beef. It settles the issue once for all: there is no beef in the Vedas.

The video is titled, *Myth of the Holy Cow and Beef in Hinduism.*[9]

---

9   https://www.youtube.com/watch?v=ecCPLt5rE58

Chapter 38

The Caste Question

IN THE 1980s, I spent time in Shantivanam, a Christian ashram on the banks of River Kaveri. Once during afternoon tea, I heard a young priest say, 'We need to make the lower castes aware of how terribly they were treated by the Brahmins.' At that time, I knew little about India, yet I interjected and asked, 'Why do you want to do this? What does it help them, if they start nurturing a grudge or even hatred for Brahmins?'

Later, I realised that such an 'awareness campaign' indeed doesn't help the lower castes, but it helps missionaries who are on a conversion spree in Bharat. The Left eco-system also, is also interested to 'spread awareness about the oppressive caste system. It's easy to get funds for such 'studies' and campaigns.

My reply in an interview on my opinion about the caste system:

In my view, the caste system is unfairly misused to demonise India and Hinduism. A genuine study of history shows that it has been misrepresented, especially by the British, probably with the agenda to convince Hindus and the world that their tradition needs to be replaced with the 'true religion'.

All over the Western world, children hear in schools that the core of Hinduism is an oppressive caste system (apart from the many Gods), which of course, is not true. I had also heard of this in primary school.

As if other societies are equal....
When I came to India, I started wondering why Indian society is so harshly condemned for 'not being equal,' as if societies elsewhere are. And why is Hinduism blamed for it, when the Vedic varna system is a horizontal, not vertical, structure of society, and caste is basically a colonial invention (it comes from the Portuguese word, *casta*).

Moreover, are people not aware that the caste system has been abolished since Independence? The 'lower castes' were given many privileges—so much so that some 'higher caste' groups even demanded to be downgraded on the social ladder so they could avail of those privileges? Where else does this happen?

Are people not aware that only the accusation of having insulted a Dalit, results in arrest? Are they not aware that in India, a former President, Chief Justice, and Chief Minister were Dalits? That the present President of India in 2025, Droupadi Murmu is from a tribal community? Where else in the world does it happen that those belonging to the so-called lowest strata of society reach the highest government offices?

Reverse discrimination
Don't people know about the reservations in Government jobs and educational institutes? Dalit students even need lower marks to get entry or admission. It has reached a point where it has become a case of reverse discrimination.

Imagine the pain of a student who has much higher marks but doesn't get a seat in an educational institution because he belongs to the so-called 'forward' caste, while his family may be much poorer than that of his so-called 'backward caste' friend? Such cases are not rare.

The least violent society is made to look the worst.
In other societies, the present generation is not held accountable for the sins of their ancestors. All over the world, terrible cruelties were committed by Christians and Muslims to indigenous people, and also by Jews who were behind the Russian revolution with its horrifying gulags. Those cruelties are documented. The sufferings of the victims were unimaginable, and the killings run into hundreds of millions.

Can historians show that upper caste Hindus killed even 'only' a hundred thousand of lower caste Hindus for belonging to the lower caste? Or, for that matter, can they show that Hindus killed non-Hindus for being non-Hindus? They cannot, because it did not happen.

Yet every new generation of Hindus is unfairly beaten with the stick of the caste system. Unfortunately, many Hindus take the stick and flog themselves for the alleged 'atrocities' which their forefathers are accused of, but which never happened— certainly not the type of atrocities for which even today, Islamic terror groups are infamous, and which intriguingly, are generously overlooked.

The traditional four-fold structure of Indian society into *varnas* was not based on birth but on inclination and profession. Usually, children took up the professions of their parents. In earlier times, it happened all over the world (and has several advantages), but the *Manu Smriti* says that one's *varna* can be changed by consistent conduct which fits another varna.

In the times of the Corona virus, I hinted in a tweet that untouchability may have had its origin in hygiene. Much to my astonishment, my tweet provoked furious reactions from all sides. It was clearly an overreaction, as hygiene might indeed have been a reason. There are rules even within Hindu families. For example, somebody, who has not yet taken his bath, must not touch the one who has already finished his. It seems that 'social distancing' was the greatest fault that the British could find with Hindus, and so they made it look really bad.

The British made sure that every Hindu was categorised into a specific 'caste' in the census, and often the census officer told the Hindus to which caste they belonged (their occupation), when they themselves did not know. In his book, *Caste, Conversion A Colonial Conspiracy*, Pt Satish K Sharma quotes an Englishman M L Middleton: 'We pigeon-holed everyone by caste and if we could not find a true caste for them, we labelled them with the name of hereditary occupation. We deplore the Caste System… but we are largely responsible for the system we deplore.'

Basically, caste is redundant in today's times where nobody knows the caste of the person who sits next to him in a bus or plane. In every society, there are jobs which are regarded higher than others. Jobs like cleaning the sewers also need to be done (maybe soon to be done by robots) and we all need to be grateful to those who do them, and definitely not look down on them.

Looking down on those who have a lower status in society is unfortunately a human trait everywhere, which needs to be overcome. It has nothing to do with Hinduism. On the contrary, only Hindu Dharma claims that the essence (Brahman) is the same in all and is divine. Moreover, in one's next life, the role one plays will be different, depending on one's *karma*.

My personal experience with 'caste discrimination', was only that we foreigners were given a separate place for eating the *prasadam* (sanctified food) in one particular ashram, which was run by orthodox Bengali Brahmins—surely a tiny snub, compared to what Hindus had to endure.

Nobody stopped me from listening to the Vedas, chanting the *Gayatri Mantra* and other sacred hymns. And in case someone claims that Hindus still discriminate against others, whereas Christians and Muslims have reformed and see all as equal, please have a closer look at what's actually happening.

In 2024, Andrew Blinken, the former US Secretary of State said at the Munich Security Conference, 'The greatest poison is dehumanisation. We need to call out dehumanisation wherever it comes from.'

Yet, he and others constantly overlook the doctrines of the Abrahamic religions (including his own, Judaism), which automatically give 'outsiders' a subhuman status. Compare this with the Hindu philosophy which claims that ultimately, we all reach back home and merge in Brahman, the universal blissful Consciousness.

From my own impression, especially in my early years in the 1980s, the greatest discrimination in India was from those with a higher job position, wealth, and fluency in English (independent of their caste) towards the poor and uneducated (independent of their caste). After Independence, Indian officials may have genuinely believed, that 'superiors' need to behave arrogantly and dismissively towards their 'subordinates', not realising that the British behaved so badly only in the colonies but couldn't do the same at home.

The continued attacks on the 'Indian Caste System' may have one more reason. Like the joint family, the caste also, apart from imparting skills and knowledge, provided a sense of belonging and security. Western society has become very lonely. Single households are common. I hope that Indian society won't become as lonesome and individualised as the West. Attempts to break the Indian family system are surely on.

Chapter 39

The Brahmin Debate

THIS WAS a question on Quora to which I had replied in August 2017. It got 237,800 views and 16,000 upvotes, yet on 18 July 2019, I got a message that it violates their 'Be nice, be respectful' policy. I appealed, but my appeal was rejected.

Please check for yourself if it is disrespectful and not nice....

Here is my reply:

Why should Brahmins feel guilty? They should feel proud. It is because of them, that India and the world still has at least a part of this most precious wisdom that is contained in the Vedas, because they painstakingly memorised them and passed them on over many thousands of years.

I guess the questioner had the caste system in mind. I am aware that the whole world knows about the caste system. Children in Germany, and surely elsewhere, too, have heard about the Indian caste system, and especially about untouchables. Pictures were shown of poor, miserable looking untouchables. The impression was given that nothing could be worse than that. This impression is not only wrong but has a mischievous agenda.

I know I tread dangerous ground now, as being a foreigner, some people even with Brahmin names may attack me for not knowing anything about the ground realities in India. All over the world, the atmosphere is vitiated with 'anti-Brahmanism' especially in the Left.

Yes, the caste or class system exists, and untouchables, too. And it exists all over the world.

Fact is that for purity, Brahmins have to stick to many more rules than any other group, as Brahmins were the guardians of the purity of the Vedas. I knew a Brahmin lady who would not enter her kitchen before taking a bath. Moreover, the four varnas—Brahmins, Kshatriyas, Vaisyas, Shudras—are meant to be a horizontal structure of society, not vertical or hierarchical, as Western societies were traditionally structured.

So, why is there such a hue and cry worldwide over the structure of Indian society, when nobody accuses for example, the royalty, the highest caste in Europe that it does not mingle with workers? More so, since Independence, India has taken so many affirmative and proactive actions in favour of the lower castes, that today, Brahmins suffer and are unfairly treated.

Why is nobody upset that the British had a board with 'Dogs and Indians not allowed' at the entrance of the club of Madikeri town in Karnataka, as an old Indian gentleman told me, and also, probably all over the country?

Why is nobody upset that the agriculture policy of the British starved over 25 million Indians to death? There are absolutely terrible pictures on the net of Indians only being skin and bones, barely alive. Each one dying a slow death, while the Britishers feasted or diverted food supplies to their troops during World War 2.

Why is nobody upset that after the slave system was abolished, the British sent indentured labour from India to all over the world, in cramped vessels and a large number of them died during the journey (perhaps that was better for they were spared the torture of working in the sugarcane estates)?

Why does nobody talk about what the Muslim invasions did to Hindus and especially to Brahmins? How cruel were they? How many Hindus were tortured, killed, or made slaves? How many Hindu Rajput women committed mass suicide (*Jauhar*) by jumping together into a huge fire so that they don't fall into the hands of the Muslim troops? Stop for a moment and imagine, how much strength and courage it needs to do this!

We can well imagine what happened then, yet Left 'activists' and even 'respectable' British Parliamentarians don't appear concerned with all this. They are only concerned with the 'terrible, most inhuman caste system' of India. Caste is not even an Indian, but a Portuguese word, and it can be safely assumed that the colonial masters tried their best to drive a wedge between the castes—successfully, as it turns out.

My point is: what Brahmins did by segregating from others or even snubbing others is negligible in comparison to what Christian colonialists and Muslim invaders did.

How many people from lower castes were killed or tortured by Brahmins? And if an individual Brahmin did indeed kill someone, he certainly did not have the sanction for his action from the Vedas.

So, why are the so-called atrocities of the caste system and especially by Brahmins, so hyped? The reason may be to divide Indian society also on caste lines, apart from the already existing religious divide. The British were masters of the divide and rule policy.

But this may not be the only reason.

Another important reason may be to make Brahmins feel guilty and to make them reluctant to follow their original calling of memorising and teaching the Vedas.

The goal is to make Vedic knowledge disappear from India, because it poses a danger for Christianity, Islam, and communism. Vedic knowledge makes sense and is therefore, the greatest obstacle for those who want fearful, weak humans who can be easily controlled.

It is about time that the world stops Brahmin-bashing; it happens even inside Bharat, especially in Tamil Nadu. Some time ago, I saw an old Brahmin couple in a temple in Puducherry. They had dignity, but were very thin. When *prasad* (sanctified food) was distributed, they were in the queue before me. Later, I saw them again in the queue.... I suspect, it was due to poverty.

No, Brahmins don't need to feel guilty. Others need to feel guilty, who scheme against India, but those others are brazen and won't feel any guilt.

Chapter 40

Dharma vs. Secularism

I DIDN'T know what great opportunities to practice equanimity I had missed, till I got a TV set in 2012. What intense emotions while listening to the different panellists on the news channels! Slowly I learned to relax and even to admire their amazing capability to listen to their opponent, and at the same time, shout at him.

No doubt, the anchors and panellists are intelligent; nevertheless they got some points consistently wrong. One such point was 'secular' or 'secularism'.

This compelled me to write the following article, 'Indian secularism is not secular' in 2013.

Meanwhile, many Indians agreed with what I had to say. They even spelt the word, secular, often as 'sickular'! On the ground, there is not much change. The dogmatic religions are still privileged over the original Hindu Dharma. This unfortunately, makes it more difficult for members of those religions who would like to return home to their original Hindu Dharma. It would mean that they would have to give up their special position as 'minorities'.

Since secularism is mentioned almost daily in the Indian media and since it is a Western 'invention', maybe I can put it into perspective:

Contrary to the general perception in India, 'secular' is not the opposite of 'communal'. Communal, as such, is not objectionable either. It means 'pertaining to a community'. In Germany, elections to local bodies are called 'communal elections' (*Kommunalwahlen*).

Secular means 'worldly' and is opposite to religious. Now, in this context, 'religious' refers to Christianity, to a well-organised, dogmatic religion that claims that it alone has the full truth, which God himself has revealed to his Church.

And what is this revealed truth?

That human beings are born in sin, which dates back to the original sin committed by Adam and Eve. But fortunately, some 2,000 years ago, God had mercy on humanity and sent his only son, Jesus Christ to earth, to redeem us from sin by dying on the cross, then rising from the dead, and going back to his Father up in heaven. However, to be able to get the benefit of Jesus' sacrifice, one must be baptised and become a member of the Church, otherwise, on Judgment Day, one will be singled out by the Almighty for eternal hell.

Understandably, such claims did not appeal to those who sought logic in the story. But for many centuries, they had to keep quiet or risk their lives. The reason was that for long, the Church was intertwined with the State, and harsh laws made sure that people did not question the 'revealed truth'. Heresy was punished with torture and death.

Significantly, those centuries, when the Church and State were intertwined, when the clergy prospered and the faithful sheep suffered, are referred to as the Dark Ages. There is a saying in Germany, which shows that the common man knew what was going on. It is summed up in this one sentence: The King said to the Pope: 'You keep them stupid. I keep them poor.'

The time, when the Church was finally forced to loosen its grip, is referred to as the Age of Enlightenment, a period which began some 350 years ago. Incidentally, India's Vedic wisdom played a big role in weaning away the intellectual elite in Europe from the Church and in fostering the progress of science.

Several persons then dared to oppose the stranglehold of religion. Many went to prison for doing so, like Voltaire who considered the Vedas as the greatest gift to humanity. 'We are eternally indebted to India,' he said.

Slowly, the idea took root that reason, and not blind belief in an unverifiable story that was centered on a historical person, should guide society, and this led to the demand for separation between the State and the Church. It meant that the State was blind towards the religion of its citizens. Such separation came to be known as secularism and is a relatively recent phenomenon in the West.

Today, most Western democracies are 'secular' and the Church cannot push her agenda through the State's power, though most Western democracies still grant preferential treatment to Christianity. For example, in Germany, the Christian doctrine is taught in government schools. The German State also collects tax for the Church from Christian citizens. Nevertheless, the present situation is a huge improvement over the Dark Ages.

Though Islam is similar to Christianity in the sense that it similarly demands belief in a story centered around a historical person, to whom the 'only truth' was revealed, secularism has little chance, as Islamic scriptures regulate religious as well as the political life. The king and the Pope –the political and the religious head–cannot be separated. If Islamic texts are followed, then a Muslim majority state is bound to be a theocracy.

However, in India, the situation is very different from Christian and Muslim countries. Here, the dominant faith of the Indian people never had a power centre that dictated unreasonable dogmas and which needed to be propped up by blasphemy laws. Their faith is based on insights of the rishis and on reason, intuition, and direct experience. It expresses itself in a multitude of ways.

Indian faith is about trust, reverence, and ultimately love for the One Source of all life. It is about doing the right thing at the right time according to one's conscience. It is about The Golden Rule: not to do to others what one does not wish to be done to oneself. It is about having noble thoughts. It is about how to live life in an ideal way.

However, this open, noble environment got a jolt when Islamic and Christian invaders entered Bharat. Indians, who good-naturedly considered the whole world as a family, were despised, ridiculed, and under Muslim rule, killed in large numbers only because they were Hindus and not Muslims.

Indians did not realise that dogmatic religions were very different from their own, ancient dharma. For the first time, they were confronted with merciless killing in the name of God. Voltaire had rightly observed, 'Those who can make you believe absurdities, can make you commit atrocities'.

Guru Nanak left a testimony in the Granth Sahib on how bad the situation was, when he cried out in despair: 'Having lifted Islam to the head, You have engulfed Hindustan in dread…. Such cruelty they have inflicted, and yet Your mercy remains unmoved….' (*Mahla* 1.360).

During Muslim rule, Hindus had to lie low for fear of their lives, and during British rule they were ridiculed by missionaries, and cut off from their traditions with the help of 'education'. Naturally, this took a toll on their self-esteem. Till today, low self-esteem especially among the English-educated class is somewhat evident. Nevertheless, it is a great achievement that Hindu Dharma has survived for so many centuries, whereas, in a short span of time, the West succumbed completely to Christianity and over fifty countries fell to Islam.

Let's come back to secularism.
Though Hindu Dharma survived and never dictated terms to the State, the word 'secular' was first added to the Constitution of India in 1976. There might have been a reason for it, because since Independence, several non-secular decisions had been taken. For example, Muslim and Christian representatives had pushed for special civil laws and other benefits and had got them.

However, after adding the word 'secular' to the Constitution, the situation did not improve. In fact, the government seemed rather eager to benefit specifically the dogmatic religions, which secularism was meant to counter.

This is inexplicable. Why would the word 'secular' be added and then not acted upon? Did Indians get the definition of secularism wrong?

Do they wrongly believe that 'secular' means fostering those two big religions which have no respect for Hindus and whose dogmas condemn all of them to eternal hell?

It is ironical and sad that Islam and Christianity that have gravely harmed Indians over the centuries get preferential treatment by the Indian state, and their own beneficial dharma that has no other home except the Indian subcontinent, is egged out.

Many Hindus 'respect' dogmatic religions, though this respect cannot be reciprocated, as long as those religions claim that their God wants everyone to worship only Him, exclusively. A religion that uses God as a front to achieve hegemony, does not become sacred; rather, it becomes dangerous. Naturally, it wants Hindu Dharma to disappear.

Media and politicians further muddy the water and call parties that represent Muslims, 'secular', instead of 'religious'. When the State gave in to the demands by Christians and Muslims, it was (falsely, of course) called 'secular'. Why did the government do this? Did it want to give its citizens a firsthand experience of what the Dark Ages were like?

Fortunately, in recent times, more and more Indians have realised that they have got the definition of 'secularism' wrong. 'Justice for all, and appeasement for none, independent of their belief,' is the true meaning of being secular.

However, Western secular nations are no role models, either. There is a lot of depression, drug abuse, alcohol, and people are generally not happy in spite of doing everything to 'enjoy life'.

Here, India has an advantage over the West as she has a great, ancient heritage in dealing with how to live life in an ideal way, and how to conduct, among other pursuits, education, economy, politics, and management.

If India becomes a nation that is based on her ancient dharma, she has good chances of regaining her position as the wealthiest and most advanced country in the world, whose citizens are open-minded and content. And, it can then take up its role as *Jagatguru*—guiding humanity towards true knowledge which is so sorely lacking in our times.

Chapter 41

Indian Influence on German Philosophers

IN THE *eighteenth and nineteenth centuries, Germany was regarded as the land of 'poets and thinkers'. One doesn't hear this now. Yet in a recent podcast, the Swiss historian Daniele Ganser used this phrase for Germans. And then he added, 'apart from Germany, India also had great thinkers and great wisdom.'*

When I heard him mention India, I wondered: Were Germans seen as great thinkers, because they had benefitted from Indian knowledge? Many of those early German philosophers recognised the brilliance of Vedantic thought and praised India's wisdom. Yet today, the Indian influence is hardly ever mentioned.

German scientists also benefitted from Indian knowledge. I wrote about this influence in one of my blogs.

Germans became interested in India rather late, but when they finally got acquainted with ancient Indian manuscripts and their translations, they became *very* interested in India.

Heinrich Heine, (1797–1856), a German author, wrote after listening to lectures on the Upanishads, 'The Portuguese, Dutch, and British have for a long time ferried huge treasures on big ships from India to their home countries. We Germans had to look on. But we will not be left behind. We take their knowledge. Our Sanskrit scholars provide us with this wealth from India right here in Bonn or Munich.'

Many German intellectuals became great admirers of India. Those early Germans never travelled to India. They knew India only from those ancient texts. They knew the profound philosophy of the Upanishads, the Bhagavad Gita, the Ramayana, and even *Shakuntala* by Kalidasa. For them, India became the land of their dreams, where beautiful people and lush nature were in harmony, and where the soul, which had gone dry in Europe, found plenty of nourishment.

The philosopher Arthur Schopenhauer (1788–1860) called Indians 'the most noble and most ancient people', and the Upanishads, 'the greatest gift of this century'. He said, 'Reading the Upanishads is comforting in my life and will be comforting when I die.'

He also wrote: 'Our religion (Christianity) will never ever take roots in India.... On the contrary, Indian wisdom will stream to Europe and will fundamentally change our knowledge and thinking.'

Max Mueller did great harm to India as a young, well-paid employee of the British East India Company. His job was to translate the Vedas, and he was eager to show that the Vedas are worthless and Christianity is much superior. Moreover, he proposed without any archaeological evidence the Aryan Invasion Theory, which helped the British to divide and rule India.

However, the older Max Mueller seemed to have realised the depth of the ancient Indian traditions and praised India highly. He said the famous sentences in his lecture at Cambridge:

'If I were asked, under what sky has the human mind most fully developed some of its choicest gifts, has most deeply pondered on the greatest problems of life, and has found solutions, I should point to India.'

'If I were asked, from which literature, we here in Europe would get refinement, which we need most to make our life more universal, inclusive, and perfect..., I would again point to India.'

Many more Germans deserve to be mentioned:

For example, the historian and philosopher Gottfried Herder (1744–1803), who took the side of the Hindus in a fictional dialogue with a missionary, in spite of the fact (or maybe, because) he had also studied theology. In his lectures on philosophy, he saw in India the 'Cradle of Humanity in a Golden Age'.

Or, the Schlegel brothers (born in 1767 and 1772), of whom the elder one established the first printing press in Devanagari script in Bonn with the help of the Prussian King.

Or, Herman Hesse (1877–1962), who wanted to visit India but reached only Ceylon, when he fell ill. He wrote the famous novel, *Siddhartha*.

Or, Friedrich Nietzsche (1844–1900), who is famous for claiming that 'God is dead'. Yet, even Friedrich Nietzsche praised India's 'religion'. He wrote, 'in regard to religion, Europe has not reached the subtleness of thought of the ancient Brahmins'.

Graf von Keyserling was one of the first who travelled to India after the Suez Canal opened. He wrote a book on Yoga, which was a big hit in the 1920s after WW1. He wrote: 'It is incredible, how important even short, but regular meditation is for inner growth.'

However, one German philosopher, Hegel (1770–1831), considered Indian philosophy as being devoid of merit. Not only this, he also claimed that the character of Indians is 'cunning and deceitful and that moral and human dignity are missing'. He was especially harsh on Brahmins: 'The British say that they only eat and sleep,' he wrote.

He was never in India, but believed the British...and yet he is praised as one of the greatest philosophers. Shouldn't his gullible attitude, to trust the British oppressors' opinion, disqualify him from being regarded as a great intellectual?

Immanuel Kant (1724–1804), another famous German philosopher, did not demean India, but rarely mentioned Indian philosophy in his lectures.

Are these two the preferred philosophers, who are today also taught to Indian students because they did not praise the Indian worldview?

Let us examine the plight of the Church.

To keep her flock under control, the Church needed to prevent Indian thought from spreading among the common people and more important, it had to be seen as primitive. They found it convenient to label Hindus as heathens.

The Church was successful in vilifying Hindus and their tradition. Even today, most people associate India and Hinduism with mainly 'an oppressive caste system and idol worship of many strange gods'. It tallies with what I had learnt in school about Hinduism decades ago.

It is a great irony that many Indian texts were looted from India by missionaries.

Missionaries were already in India long before curiosity and longing for India gripped German thinkers. For example, Heinrich Roth (born 1620), a Jesuit, was the first German

Sanskrit scholar. He died in Agra in 1668 as head of the Jesuit Residency. A few years earlier, he had visited Germany and Italy. Did he 'donate' Indian texts to the Vatican and German libraries, like the missionary Haeberl did to the Tuebingen University later in 1839?

The Dean of Tuebingen University praised the 'gift' of 11 volumes of ancient Indian texts from Haeberl, as a 'great ornament for the university' and added—'of course, our treasure is small compared to the treasure which is in the India House in London.'

The Dean made this statement four years after Thomas Macauley, had in 1835, introduced the English school system in India, designed to tell Indian students that their tradition is worthless and half a shelf of English literature has more worth than all their literature put together.

It was an insidious ploy to appropriate and benefit from Indian knowledge and at the same time, cut Indians off from it and make them look down upon it.

Fortunately, there is a certain revival now of traditional Indian thought.

Now, many Indians are learning Sanskrit and are taking interest in knowing more about the vast Indian Knowledge System (IKS), where still millions of texts have not been studied. This revival may be a reason why nowadays great care is taken NOT to mention 'India' in any positive way. For example, while those Germans in earlier centuries acknowledged the valuable inspiration they got from India, modern Western philosophers don't acknowledge that they make use of Indian thought in 'their own' philosophy, such as the concept of maya.

In future, perhaps Elon Musk will be seen as having

discovered the concept of maya. He said recently that this world is not the real thing and that it is more like virtual reality. Out of all fairness, shouldn't he be acknowledging the origin of this insight? After all, it's the West which started copyrights and patents and is regularly suing people for plagiarism.

India always gave freely. Maybe too freely to the wrong people.

◉◉◉

Note:
All quotes by different philosophers have been translated by the author from the book: *Sehnsucht nach Indien*, by Veena Kade-Luthra, Verlag Beck, 1993

Chapter 42

Should Indians Stress on Their Sufferings like the Jews Do?

INDIANS ARE generally good-natured. Their dharmic mind-set makes them like this. They did not patent their vast knowledge, because they know that this knowledge came from the One Source from where everything originates. They see the whole world as their family, but had to painfully realise that many others don't share their worldview, or rather, lack those deep insights.

Surely, there are no other people on earth who have suffered as much as Indians have done during the last thousand years—first under Muslim invaders and then under colonial rule. A recent study shows that under British rule between 100 to 165 million Indians had perished.[10] Add to this the brutality of the Muslims towards Hindus, who even felt proud about making towers with decapitated Hindu heads!

---

[10] https://geopoliticaleconomy.com/2022/12/12/britain-100-million-india-deaths-colonialism/

Further, the foreigners who came to India made the once richest country into one of the poorest. The loot was monumental. Here again, Britain stands out. An Oxfam study speaks of USD 65 trillion that were looted through trade. On top of this, how many thousand tons of gold disappeared from India, of course nobody knows. This study also mentions that the top 10 per cent of British society kept over half of this loot, almost USD 34 trillion[11]. Imagine what those ultra-rich families, who are still around, can do to our world even today!

One would expect British politicians, if not regretful, to at least not make false accusations against India. Yet this does not happen and British politicians continue to make baseless accusations against India.

Why? Are they convinced that their education policy worked and that Indians have internalised that they are inferior and cannot expect to be treated equally? And, have Hindus camouflaged this attitude as some 'moral high ground' of not playing the victim card?

Many Hindus see themselves in a similar position as Jews, because both groups were persecuted over centuries. Yet, while the Jews keep reminding everyone of their persecution through movies, books, memorial days, and by getting laws enacted in other countries, besides having numerous powerful groups which monitor the slightest discrimination against their own people, many Hindus say that we should forget the past and move on.

---

11   https://economictimes.indiatimes.com/news/india/uk-extracted-64-82-trillion-from-india-during-colonial-rule-richest-10-got-most-of-the-cash/articleshow/117394631.cms

This has been counterproductive because it's unbelievable, but true: Hindus, the most open-minded and most tolerant group of people, now stand accused as oppressors!

The latest report from 2025, of the US Commission for Religious Freedom, again lists India as a country of special concern for persecuting Christians. India is ranked right after Afghanistan and before Saudi Arabia and Syria. The commissioners, who decided on the listing were Christians, Jews, and Muslims.

It's not for the first time that such false accusations have been made about India. The article reproduced in this chapter refers to the same report on Religious Freedom from 2019, which a British government official had released. Obviously, Britain has no shame about what they did to India.

Media is no longer about disseminating information. It probably never was. It is about influencing opinions to promote the agenda of certain interests, and lies are an accepted tool for it.

Lies are often disguised as surveys or even research. Nobody would believe lies if they were too obvious. Yet when a World Watch List, for example by Open Doors in England, gives out a ranking on the level of persecution of Christians in the world, and when the report is released by none other than the British Foreign Secretary, Jeremy Hunt in January 2019 who also tweets about it, then the ranking acquires respectability and credibility, even if it contains plain falsehoods. So, from now on, people who would have heard about this list will 'know' that the level of persecution of Christians is extremely high in India, higher than for example in Syria or Nigeria.

Clearly, this list falls under propagating falsehood in the name of an agenda. There is no other country where the members of other religions are as safe as in India. Hindus have always given shelter to those who were persecuted in their homelands. Jews acknowledged that India is the one country where they were never persecuted. Syrian Christians under their leader, Thomas of Cana (Thomas the Apostle did not come to India as is popularly believed) were given refuge in the fourth century. Parsis came in the tenth century to escape the Muslim invaders in Persia. And, in 1959, some 100,000 Tibetan Buddhists fled over the high Himalayan mountains and found shelter in India—barely twelve years after the British had left the country that was one of the richest when they seized power and one of the poorest, when they left.

Yet, now the British Foreign Secretary had tweeted that nobody should be persecuted for his faith and obviously endorsed the ranking of India in the 'extreme level' category at number 10 out of 50 countries.

Of course, nobody should be persecuted for his faith. Yet an important issue is overlooked. What is the reason for persecution? Who is likely to persecute others for their faith?

Naturally, it must be those who believe in an ideology which considers the faith of those others as wrong and unacceptable.

There exist three such ideologies—Communism, Christianity, and Islam whose followers have not only persecuted, but over centuries killed in millions those who did not subscribe to their views.

Communism wants to stamp out belief in God as it considers it a disease. It started its experiment in Russia with disastrous consequences for Orthodox Christian Russians.

Islam wants to obliterate all other faiths except itself, and likewise Christianity. Both consider all other faiths as false and unacceptable to their God, and therefore, are prone to persecute them.

So, the first countries on the list may indeed deserve their rank and indeed persecute Christians. North Korea due to its communism, and then right up to rank 17, all are Muslim majority countries with one exception. Rank number 10 lists India which has a Hindu majority.

How did India get in there? There seems to be an agenda to muddle the issue. Hinduism does not condemn other faiths as wrong and does not persecute others. It has the most open-minded worldview. Everyone is allowed to search for the Absolute Truth and to connect with the Ultimate Source in their own way.

So why is India ranked together with countries where Christians are indeed persecuted? Surely the compilers of the list must have a reason to include India? Was not a young American missionary killed by tribals in the Andaman Islands recently? And, is this not brutal persecution?

Yes, it is true. He was killed. The young American was naïve. He knew that the Sentinelese tribe was cut off from civilisation and hostile, and nobody was allowed to go there. Yet, he nevertheless went, feeling that he was called upon to bring the Gospel to them, as if they were in need of it. His superiors should have warned him, but they didn't and in that sense, encouraged a possible 'martyrdom'.

But this unfortunate incident definitely cannot be called persecution of Christians. It was a defence against an unwanted intruder by the tribals, who had earlier had bad experiences under British colonial rule.

It also cannot be called persecution of Christians, when occasionally, villagers chased away missionaries who had come to convert them. These villagers had every right to tell them that they are not welcome and must leave. And if there is some pushing and shoving from the villagers' side, the Christians surely cannot cry 'persecution'. Missionaries are notorious for crossing decent human behaviour. They call Hindu Gods 'devils' and pester Hindus to leave their ancient tradition by trying to lure them with material benefits or by frightening them with talk about hellfire.

They have powerful organisations and a lot of money to back them. And they put out blatantly fake news to suit their purposes. Here is one example:

Swiss friends of mine were alarmed by a forward they had received on 23 November 2018 and asked me if there was any truth in it. It was in German and I translate it here in full:

SAD NEWS: Please pray! Urgent issue for prayers. Pray for the Church in India. Last night, twenty churches were burnt down. And tonight, more than 200 churches in the Olisabang province are meant to be destroyed. They want to kill 200 missionaries in the next twenty-four hours. All Christians hide in villages.... Pray for them and send this message to all Christians whom you know the world over. Pray to God that He has mercy for our brothers and sisters in India. When you receive this message, pass it on urgently to other people. Please pray for the twenty-two Christian missionary families who have been condemned to be executed. Please pass on this message as fast as you can, so that many will pray!!!

With love
Joyce Meyer

A Google search shows that this message is circulating since 2010 and is a hoax. Even the province does not exist.

Would a persecuted religious group dare to spread such outrageous lies? Would it dare to have a detailed plan like the

Joshua Project about how to convert a maximum number of Hindus? So, who is actually persecuting whom?

Yet, instead of condemning the devious agenda of missionaries, the world accuses India of persecuting Christians. Mainstream media has tremendous power to shape opinions. Churches have tremendous financial and political clout. Both portray Hindus as intolerant and hateful of other religions—which is absolutely contrary to the facts.

Intriguingly, not a single European or American country is among the 50 top countries where Christians are persecuted.

But was there not a shooting in a church in the USA? Have not Christian refugees been recently attacked by Muslim refugees in Germany? Does this not count as persecution? And, are those French or German or Spanish or English citizens, who are randomly stabbed with a knife or blown up in a terror attack, not targeted for their faith? For not being Muslims?

We need to be clear. Those who are persecuted FOR their faith, are always persecuted by members of a different faith which is rigid and dogmatic and considers those other views as wrong—so wrong that they are ready to even cheat or kill to wipe out this wrong faith.

So, in a tweet to the British Foreign Secretary, I suggested a slight change in his comment. Instead of 'Nobody should be persecuted FOR his faith' I suggested, 'Nobody should be persecuted BY a faith'.

Will he understand?

Chapter 43

If Only All Humans had the Inclusive Hindu Mindset

IN THE end a reminder about the solid philosophical basis of Hindu Dharma and why it is superior to the dogmatic Abrahamic religions, which, apart from the belief in a Higher Power, are based on blind belief in dogmas. Some of those dogmas make absolutely no sense and have proven very harmful for humanity, like the dogma that 'others' are inferior and will be damned for eternity.

Recently, a friend asked, 'What is Sanatana Dharma according to you?'

Sanatana Dharma is so vast. How to put it briefly? Let me try:

Sanatana means 'eternal' and dharma basically means 'to do what is right in a given situation; to do one's duty'.

How do we know what is right? In most cases, our conscience tells us what is right, unless we have internalised some absurd philosophies, like moral relativism where there is no right or wrong and no justice. Or, if we have grown up in one of the three Abrahamic religions and have been indoctrinated from childhood that 'others' are inferior and, therefore, they don't deserve the same considerations like 'our own people'.

Yet, without those artificial distortions, the great majority of the human population is equipped with a moral barometer which generally points them towards the right direction.

But, is the main thing in life to be an honest, upright, compassionate human being?

It is a very important part, because on this basis, the most important other aspect of Sanatana Dharma can be understood: Being honest and following one's conscience makes one receptive to the finer layers of consciousness, and such refinement is necessary to understand and realise the truth.

And, to realise the truth about us and the universe is the other very important aspect of Sanatana Dharma.

The Vedas, Upanishads, and innumerable other ancient Indian texts contain wisdom which a human being cannot easily discover. This wisdom was 'seen' by the rishis and was never proven wrong.

The main point of this wisdom is:

You are one with limitless, pure Consciousness. You are like a wave on the ocean of Consciousness. And of course, the wave is one with the ocean. Another description for this foundational Consciousness is 'unconditional Love'—but ultimately, all words fall short.

Anandamayi Ma put it like this: 'You are never forsaken. You never need to fear. You are forever in Bhagawan's loving embrace.'

Yes, it needs great trust to realise this. To realise that God is truly within. There are many distractions on the way. But this truth has not only been confirmed by enlightened masters, but also by those who had temporary insights into a different state of consciousness or had near-death experiences.

It follows naturally that the goal of life is to realise this blissful Oneness, to 'know' it as clearly as one now knows that one is a human being and not a dog.

Plenty of tips are given on how to discover this Oneness. The Bhagavad Gita is probably the best guide; it explains *Jnana Yoga, Bhakti Yoga*, and *Karma Yoga*.

Jnana Yoga approaches unity (*yog* means to join) through knowledge, by deeply reflecting on what is true and identifying with that again and again. Bhakti Yoga aspires to unite with that inner Presence through one's feelings, by keeping in touch with its divine forms through *japa* and prayers, and by developing deep love for it - and finally merging with it in love. Karma Yoga, the path of action, tries to erase one's ego by doing all actions to the best of one's ability, but without expecting certain results. All actions are dedicated to the one Supreme Being. When one's ego is erased, Truth shines through.

There are many more helpful means. For example, *Asthanga Yoga* and *Raja Yoga* which advise inner and outer purity, *Pranayama, Yogasanas*, meditation, but also *poojas*, temple visits, and sattvic food among others.

Sanatana Dharma gives great freedom to find the way back to our eternal, blissful home—we can choose and mix the different approaches best suited to our nature.

The experience of our divine inner core gives strength. It makes us kind to other living beings and respectful to nature. It's the ideal basis for society.

Compare this with the doctrine of the Abrahamic religions that other humans, apart from those in one's own religious group, are inferior, and that animals and nature can be exploited, because according to their holy books, man is the 'crown of creation'.

Fortunately, many Christians in the West no longer take the claims of the Church as 'gospel truth'. Many Christians now pick and choose those aspects of the doctrine that suit them and discard others—for example, after death, many want their bodies to be burned, not buried, and they believe in rebirth and not in only one life. I wished this 'pick-and-choose-what-makes-sense-attitude' would also become popular with Indian Christians, many of whom are generally strongly indoctrinated by their clergy, stronger than Christians in countries, where they are the majority.

Many of Jesus' sayings not only make sense but mirror India's ancient wisdom. His claim 'I and my Father are one' is fully in tune with Advaita Vedanta, provided, it is not ascribed ONLY to Jesus, as the Church baselessly does. For discerning Christians, Jesus Christ is a Divine, beloved guide, like Krishna or Ram is a Divine, beloved guide or avatar for Hindus. This makes those Christians more like Hindus. And indeed, a *Newsweek* article by Lisa Miller from August 2009 was titled *We are all Hindus now.* (The title was changed in 2010 to *US views on God and Life are turning Hindu*[12]).

That is great news, because it is in the interest of humanity if we all had the open, inclusive Hindu mindset. Then Christian, Muslim, and Jewish children would no longer be told: 'You are so lucky because you have been born in the true religion and God loves you. But He doesn't love those, who

---

12 https://www.newsweek.com/us-views-god-and-life-are-turning-hindu-79073

don't believe in our books, and will severely punish them.'

This teaching has been going on since centuries and needs to stop. In fact, it is incomprehensible, that no serious (and successful) attempt was made so far to stop it. Wouldn't it be easy to stop it even within one generation? It would only need the clergy of the dogmatic religions to teach their children that God or Allah wants all humans to live good, compassionate lives. And further that He loves all and wants all to come back to Him. Is this so difficult to teach? Is it easier to teach that God or Allah harbours hatred for some humans, just because they don't believe in certain books? Surely, no sane person can believe that the topmost authority and power in the universe will cast billions of humans into hell for eternal suffering!

The fact that this simple remedy to heal divisions within humanity (and the terrorists) has not been applied over many centuries, may indicate that some powers—they may be negative powers in the spiritual realm—want humans to be divided and unhappy.

But we can counter them with the help of positive spiritual powers. Let's stop identifying with religion, gender, or race—all of which are only labels for our temporary bodies. In truth, we are blissful consciousness, and bliss is just another word for love.

Instead of ignorantly asserting that we are small persons in a big world, let's dedicate our lives to uncovering the God within.

That's anyway the purpose why we are here in a physical form.